INSPIRATION
AND
AUTHORITY

INSPIRATION
AND
AUTHORITY

*Nature and Function of
Christian Scripture*

PAUL J. ACHTEMEIER

HENDRICKSON
PUBLISHERS

Copyright © 1999 by Paul J. Achtemeier
Hendrickson Publishers, Inc.
P. O. Box 3473
Peabody, Massachusetts 01961–3473
All rights reserved
Printed in the United States of America

ISBN 1-56563-363-6

First printing — June 1999

This is a revised and expanded edition of *The Inspiration of Scripture: Problems and Proposals.* © 1980 The Westminster Press, assigned 1997 Paul J. Achtemeier.

Library of Congress Cataloging-in-Publication Data

Achtemeier, Paul J.
    Inspiration and authority: nature and function of Christian
    Scripture   /   Paul J. Achtemeier.
    Includes bibliographical references and index.
    ISBN 1-56563-363-6 (pbk.)
    1. Bible—Inspiration.   I. Achtemeier, Paul J.   Inspiration of
    Scripture.   II. Title.
    BS480.A245   1999
    220.1′3—dc21   98-54748
                                                                      CIP

To the memory of my father
Arthur R. Achtemeier

a good man, now departed,
who faithfully proclaimed
the word of God

Table of Contents

Foreword

The task of writing a book on the inspiration of Scripture is a formidable task indeed, and one not to be undertaken lightly. The history of the church has shown clearly enough that to enter this realm is to enter a place where passions run high and invective is close at hand. Yet perhaps there is a place for a book that seeks to express a conviction about the inspiration of Scripture that is able to accommodate the discoveries of modern scholars of the Bible. It is that place which this book seeks to fill.

Many people have contributed to its writing, and I must thank some of them: Mrs. Martha Aycock, the reference librarian at Union Theological Seminary in Virginia, who is never baffled by a request for information, however vaguely that request may be phrased; Mrs. Ann Charlton, my secretary, who arranged and rearranged notes as necessary, even when she was not entirely clear as to why it was necessary; Union Theological Seminary in Virginia, for a sabbatical leave during which these pages were written; my wife, my true partner in the dialogue of life, who has borne up remarkably well and has offered endless encouragement and sage advice as the ideas for the book developed and were chewed and digested along with the food at many a meal; finally to the one to whom this book is dedicated, from whom I learned, through precept and example, to revere the message of the Bible, and to love its living Lord.

P. J. A.

Foreword to the Revised Edition

The positive reception accorded to the original edition of the book, particularly among evangelicals and Roman Catholic scholars, has emboldened me to send it forth a second time, equipped with some modest revisions and additions. I have profited from the judgments of reviewers; I have sought to make clearer some points where I did not express myself with sufficient precision in the earlier edition, and I have allowed to remain those points that appeared to others to have been well taken. I am grateful to Hendrickson Publishers for giving me the chance to make those revisions and to add a short chapter on authority. Arguments over the way inspiration is to be conceived among the Southern Baptists, and among some other Protestant denominations challenges to the authority of scriptural commands with respect to homosexual activities, show that the issues of inspiration and authority continue to occupy Christians in our time as they have in the past. For that reason I venture to issue this revised and expanded edition.

Introduction

That some form of doctrine concerning the inspiration of Scripture is a key issue for the Christian faith should hardly be a matter of dispute. What is at stake in that doctrine is nothing less than the question of the importance of the Bible as the source for Christian belief and action. However one may want to conceive of that inspiration, it points to the belief on the part of the church that there is a unique linkage between God's communication with humankind and that specific collection of literature. All that we know of the prophetic protest against a series of rulers content with the normal way of doing things in the ancient Semitic world we know from our Bible. Virtually all that we know reliably of the words and deeds of Jesus, who, both by what he said and by what he did, kindled in many of his contemporaries the unshakable conviction that contact with him meant in a unique and unrepeatable way contact with God himself, we know from that same Scripture. Much if not all that we know of the many events and reflections which constitute the very foundation and essence of our faith, we know from that one source. Unless that Bible can in some way claim a unique status and authority for its content and intention, the Christian faith becomes what its opponents, past and present, claim it is: a human attempt to solve human problems, suffering from the delusion that it represents something more.

If the Christian faith is to make any kind of claim to be "something more" than just another philosophy or human system projecting onto the heavens its own desires, it will have to base that claim at some point on its Scriptures. That it is justified in doing so is the burden of the doctrine of inspiration. To some extent, at least, it would be fair to say that the truth claims of the church rest on the reliability of the truth claims of its Scripture. Clearly, without its Scriptures, the Christian faith would not be what it has historically understood itself to be, nor what it continues in our day to claim that it is.

In the light of that importance, it is surprising and puzzling that discussion of the doctrine of inspiration has often been notable more by its absence than its presence. It has been honored by being ignored in many circles. Part of that silence has been due to the embarrassment of people who no longer shared the theological tenets that made a kind of "verbal inerrancy" an adequate formulation for understanding inspiration, but who were unwilling or unable to reformulate the doctrine in a way compatible with their different view of the nature of Scripture. Indeed, absence of discussion of the doctrine in any form, I suspect, has been characteristic of courses both in Bible and in doctrine in the majority of the "mainline" theological institutions over the past decade or two. Even conservative theological circles, unified largely by their insistence upon defining inspiration in terms of some form of inerrancy, have tended to speak mostly to themselves, when they spoke at all on this issue.

All of that has changed radically over the past few years, particularly in the more conservative areas. Indeed, many conservative evangelicals perceive the question of inerrancy, and the view of inspiration that best accommodates such a view, to be the key question faced by themselves and their churches and theological institutions. That the issue still contains the potential of exploding into major importance has been amply demonstrated by events that took place within the Lutheran Church–Missouri Synod in the recent past. Bitter confrontation, confusion within the denomination, and a split in a major theological seminary faculty and within the church itself have resulted from debate on this issue. The emergence of divisions within other confessional bodies and theological persuasions is also a key issue for the people affected. One need only read the evaluation of the "defection" of Fuller Seminary in Harold Lindsell's *The Battle for the Bible*, and the response by those of the Fuller faculty who share a more moderate view, as represented in the essays contained in *Biblical Authority*, edited by Jack Rogers, to be aware of the seriousness with which such divisions are being taken. The discussion has been joined in other ways from a more conservative point of view (*The Foundation of Biblical*

Authority, edited by James M. Boice) and from a more moderate stance (Stephen T. Davis, *The Debate About the Bible*) within the overall group who still hold to some form of inerrancy as the best expression of the nature of the inspiration of the Bible. The emergence of the International Council on Biblical Inerrancy, which formulated the Chicago Statement on Biblical Inerrancy, shows that the lines of debate that had already emerged late in the nineteenth century remain central for those who want to maintain the factual inerrancy of Christian Scriptures. More recently, the schisms wracking the various Southern Baptist conventions show that the question has lost none of its urgency. Once again, bitter debates, divisions within congregations and theological seminaries, and denominational confusion have been the result. The essays in such a book as *The Unfettered Word: Southern Baptists Confront the Authority-Inerrancy Question*, edited by Robison B. James, display the perennial questions, and the perennial pain, involved in such disputes. More indirectly, but nevertheless equally to the point, the discussions about the way the biblical witness concerning human sexuality is to be interpreted intersects with the way the authority, and thus the inspiration, of the Bible are to be understood. Questions of the best way to understand the inspiration of Scripture thus continue to occupy a variety of churches, as they seek to find the proper use, and hence the proper understanding, of the nature of Scripture, its inspiration, and its authority.

In the face of all of this, it is evident that reflection on the nature of the inspiration of the Bible is imperative on the part of those for whom factual inerrancy is an inadequate explanation of what is taken to be the unique sign of the difference between Christian Scriptures and all other literature. Some discussion has taken place, both from the orientation of the history of this doctrine (Bruce Vawter, *Biblical Inspiration*) and from the perspective of a theologically critical view of the conservative position (James Barr, *Fundamentalism*). Further attempts have also been made to reflect on the question of how best to understand inspiration, among them *Biblical Inspiration* by I. Howard Marshall and *The Divine Inspiration of Holy Scripture* by William J. Abraham, the former aware of the arguments proposed in the first edition of these pages. Neither of them renders superfluous, however, the reflections proposed in the following pages on the way inspiration may be understood in the light of recent discoveries about the nature of the Scripture to which the church looks for guidance, and about which it claims some form of divine inspiration. It is to that continuing task that the following pages seek to make a contribution.

Inevitably, however, reflection on inspiration immediately involves us in reflection on a whole spectrum of related problems. Intimately related to the question of the inspiration of Scripture, for example, is the question of the intention of Scripture. A perennial problem faced by all those who attempt to understand and interpret the Bible, whether professionally or for personal reasons, it centers around the task of letting the Bible speak as it wants to speak. Instead of trying to impose preconceived notions on Scripture, in which case nothing new can be learned from it, the basic problem consists in trying to listen to and understand the text in such a way that we find illumination for our lives.

Underlying that problem is another, a more vexing problem, namely, what kind of book is it to whose message we listen and from which we attempt to learn? What kind of truth does it intend to convey, and how does it intend to convey it? Light would be thrown on such a question if we could determine how and for what purposes the Scriptures were originally composed and assembled. Light would also be thrown on that question if we could determine what the Bible itself says about its own composition and intention.

At the very foundation of all of this lies the question of the relationship of the Bible to God's will for his people and his world. We need to know with some precision just what kind of literature we are dealing with when we read the Bible, and how that literature was produced and by whom, if we are to gain some leverage on the problem of how we may go about hearing God's voice speaking to us through the pages of Scripture.

These are the kinds of problems which surround and inform any attempt to think through and formulate a doctrine of the inspiration of Scripture, and it is to problems like these that this book is also addressed. This book offers no claim to solve the problem in such fashion that all reasonable men and women must be persuaded of the author's view immediately upon reading its pages. The book does not intend, in fact, to "convert" anyone to the view of the nature of the Bible, and the way we may understand its inspiration, represented in its pages. The debate between "conservatives" and "liberals" (slippery labels which we will use only because they are inevitable in this kind of discussion) which has raged for nearly a century and a half makes it clear that reasoned arguments are as unlikely to move a person from one position to the other as are other forms of persuasion, ranging from heresy trials to caustic sarcasm. Rather, this book is intended to help those who are not persuaded by the "conservatives" (their own preferred self-designation is "evangelicals") and their doctrine of total and plenary inerrancy, to formulate a view of the inspiration of Scripture that will allow the Bible to continue to play a meaningful role in their lives. It is an attempt to help them think through the problem, the evidence on which solutions must be based, and the alternative explanations of that evidence.

In pursuing such a goal, we shall from time to time have to touch on still other related problems. For example, the debate about the nature of Scripture, and the way its inspiration is to be understood, is almost as old as the church that reveres those Scriptures, and we shall from time to time refer to some episodes in that history. This book is not, however, a history of the various views of inspiration, and no attempt will be made to cover even the major historic positions of the church on this problem. There are books which do that, and they make profitable reading, but this is not such a history. Only to the extent that knowledge of such positions contributes directly to understanding the current debate will they be cited.

Nor does this book pretend to be either an exhaustive résumé of all current views or a systematic and careful evaluation of them, although a goodly number of pages will be devoted to outlining some of the current alternatives in understanding the inspiration of Scripture. Again, there are books that undertake such careful résumés and evaluations, and they too make profitable reading, but this is not one of those surveys.

Finally, although we are dealing with an issue closely connected to the question of the persuasiveness of biblical solutions to human problems, and what we say will have implications for the way we understand and acknowledge such persuasiveness, this book is not intended to demonstrate why or how the biblical "answers" ought to become authoritative for our lives as we approach the new millennium. There are books that deal with that kind of problem, and they too make useful reading. Rather, this book is intended for those who are already persuaded that the Bible aids them in making sense of their lives and who wish to find some kind of suitable intellectual explanation to themselves, and perhaps to others, that makes sense of such a conviction. That conviction will of course have other, perhaps far profounder and deeper, roots than reasoned formulas, but if such a conviction is to exercise its full influence on our lives, we must have some conception of what it is, and hence what it can mean. It is the intention of this book to present one way of understanding how the Bible may be said to be inspired and hence how it can lay a legitimate claim to speaking a persuasive word to us and to the way we carry on our lives.

In pursuing the goal of finding a useful way to state how and in what ways the Bible may be understood to be inspired, we shall first sketch the range of problems associated with this question. We shall then outline some current options for understanding what we mean when we say that the Bible is inspired. That outline will include in each case the option itself and some of the problems its opponents have found with it. The second step will be to examine the nature of Scripture itself, as that is understood by contemporary critical biblical scholars. That examination will shed further light on some of the shortcomings of some current options for understanding the inspiration of Scripture. The third step will be an investigation of some elements that must be taken into account, if our understanding of inspiration is to accord both with the nature of Scripture as we now understand it and with what the Bible itself says about its own inspiration. In the light of those elements, we shall propose a way to understand the inspiration of Scripture. A further item to be explored will be some implications such a view of Scripture and its inspiration have for the way the Bible ought to be used, and for what we can and cannot expect to learn from its pages.

Because the inspiration of Scripture and its authority are so intimately related, one cannot discuss the former without at least some attention to the latter. The final section of our discussion will therefore be devoted to the way biblical authority has been, and is now, understood. Here questions of canon and inspiration, text and truth, interpretation and history converge in the attempt to define the locus and nature of authority that can be claimed for the Bible. A number of conflicts in mainline churches, in whatever terms they may be phrased, are in fact conflicts about the nature and extent of biblical authority, demonstrating yet again the perennial importance of this topic.

In the last analysis, however, such contributions as this book may have to make to contemporary theological discussion will reside in what it has to say about the question of the inspiration of Scripture. This book remains in many ways only a preliminary sketch, and much of what is said in these pages has been said before. Yet the continuing debates on these matters make it urgent that an attempt be undertaken at a more systematic statement of the way modern scholars view Scripture, and of the implications that has for the way we understand its inspiration and view its authority.

Chapter 1

Locus and Mode
of Inspiration

Part of the common heritage in which all Christians share is the conviction that the Bible occupies a special place in the life and worship of the church and its members. To say that the Bible is "inspired" means at least that in some special way the literature in that book owes its origin to God himself and to the events behind which he has stood, which are reported in its pages, and that therefore the Bible occupies a central and irreplaceable position within the Christian faith. In a unique way our contact with the God of whom the Bible speaks is linked to the records of what that God has said and done in the past, which are contained in the Bible. The confession of faith that that is so does not limit itself to the past, however. Part of the confession that God has spoken in the past, and that we have an authoritative account of those words, also refers to the present. To say that Scripture is "inspired" means that God continues to address his people through its pages in the present. For the Christian, the "inspired" Bible means that God spoke not only to our forebears in the history of Israel, and to the apostles in the founding generation of the Christian church, but that he also continues to address his people through its pages, as they are read in public worship and private devotions. The lives of countless Christians, public and private, in secular and worship contexts, bear witness to the continuing power of the Scriptures to mediate the will of God for contemporary life.

THE SHAPE OF THE PROBLEM

If Christians share the common belief that the Bible occupies a unique place in their faith, they do not share a common understanding of the way that unique place is to be perceived. If Christians agree that in some sense God speaks to us through the accounts contained in the Scriptures, and hence that those Scriptures are inspired, all Christians do not agree as to the way that inspiration is to be described and understood.

The attempt to find an appropriate way to express their deeply held convictions about the nature of the Bible and its witness has occupied Christian thinkers almost from the beginning of the church, and with the Reformation it came to be a central issue in theological understanding and formulation. It has become clear enough in the course of those debates, and in the debates about the Bible that have continued to the present time, that the way in which inspiration is understood has wide-ranging implications for the way many other concepts in the Christian faith are to be understood. It is our task in these pages to investigate some of the ways inspiration has been understood to occur, and some of the doctrines of the Christian faith that are affected by that understanding.

Perhaps the most natural approach to our problem would be to turn to the Bible itself and see what it has to say about its own inspiration. Although some passages refer to this phenomenon, the most notable being 2 Timothy 3:16, it quickly becomes apparent that the Bible itself contains no full-blown or systematically formulated doctrine of its own significance. While the claim is made in 2 Timothy 3:16 that "all Scripture" is "God inspired" or "God inbreathed" and hence is useful for religious purposes, how that inspiration occurred is not made clear. Yet it is precisely the solution to the problem of the how of inspiration that will affect in so great a measure the way other aspects of the Christian faith are understood.

A major problem associated with the *how* of inspiration, for example, concerns the locus of that inspiration. Is it the authors of Scripture that we are to speak of as inspired, or is it the words that those authors wrote down that we are to see as bearing the major share of inspiration?[1] Both instances have been argued. How, the defenders of

---

[1] There is a good discussion of these alternative ways of understanding inspiration in J. K. S. Reid, *The Authority of Scripture* (New York: Harper & Brothers, 1957), ch. 5, 156ff.

the former position argue, can one seriously suppose that inspiration can adhere to the paper, ink, or type of these writings? Is it not much more reasonable to suppose that what we have to do with in Scripture are certain persons who have been inspired by God, persons upon whose heart or mind the Spirit first worked its influence, and who under that inspired power wrote down the words we have in our Bible? Surely the Spirit is given to the person, and from that inspiration the words then derive their authority.[2] Defenders of the latter position will counter with the question: How can we be sure that what the inspired author wrote was a true reflection of that inspiration if we cannot also say that the very words he or she put down were also inspired, shared also in the inbreathing of the divine Spirit? Is it not more realistic to believe that the influence of the Holy Spirit was at work in the very writing of the biblical authors, so that what they wrote was an authoritative account—because inspired—of what God had done for them and their times?[3] If that is not the case, then how can we realistically speak of the Scriptures as inspired?

Since too great an emphasis on the person as bearer of inspiration, on the one hand, and on the words themselves as bearer of inspiration, on the other, has led to such problems, a third possibility has also been proposed. That position would want to affirm that what is inspired is to be understood not exclusively of the person, though he or she of course shared in the inspiration, nor solely of the words written down, though they too were not unaffected by the power of God's Spirit. Rather, the content of Scripture, the thoughts that the authors sought to convey in the words they chose, is the locus of inspiration. Thus, if some of the words of a certain passage are uncertain because of damage to ancient manuscripts, all is not lost, since what is important is the sense the words sought to convey rather than the very words themselves. Again, if our contact with the inspired person is impossible because of the passage of time—we cannot have direct personal access to the Apostle Paul, for example, simply because he died centuries ago—we can nev-

---

[2] An example is James Orr, who argues for this position in *Revelation and Inspiration* (Grand Rapids: Eerdmans, 1952 reprint), 162–63.

[3] Stephen T. Davis argues for this, although not entirely in the form I have cast the discussion; see his *The Debate About the Bible* (Philadelphia: Westminster, 1977), 54, 114–15.

ertheless have access to the author's message, to the content of what the writer sought to convey through the written word.[4]

While each of these solutions that we have sketched out—inspiration located in the person, the words, or a combination of the two—has its own problems and its own strengths, all three of them share one common assumption. That assumption is that each book of Scripture was produced by an individual author, who thought about the content, organized it, and then either wrote it down or dictated it to another who wrote it down. That author is therefore the key to what has been written. The more important question, then, when dealing with the *how* of inspiration is not so much the *locus* of the inspiration—whether in person, words, or a combination—but the *mode* of inspiration. That is, how can it happen that the inspiration is mediated to the author in the first place? If inspiration means that Scripture in some way has its origin in God himself, how are we to understand that phrase *in some way?* How did God use the authors of Scripture so that what they thought and wrote bore the imprint of the divine origin and hence the divine intention? How, in sum, are we to understand the process by which God used the authors to set down in Scripture what God himself wanted set down?

There has been a great deal of discussion of this problem in the course of the life of the church, and we shall have occasion to refer to some of it in a moment. Yet there was one solution proposed, and then further refined, which has played a major role in setting the stage for modern discussions of inspiration. That classic solution was formulated during the period of the history of the church when Christian scholars found in the philosophy of Aristotle the most useful instrument for articulating Christian doctrine. That period is known as the Scholastic period, or more broadly the Middle Ages. Aristotle's thinking covered a vast range of subjects and offered a set of categories by which, so it was believed, the totality of reality could be subsumed and understood. Among those categories upon which Aristotle reflected were a number dealing with causation, and he differentiated between

---

[4] This position was espoused both by Heinrich Heppe, a Reformed scholar (cited in Reid, *The Authority of Scripture,* 43), and by Cardinal J. B. Franzelin and Christian Pesch, both nineteenth-century Jesuits, although again not exactly in the form which I have given to it. I owe the material on the Jesuits to Bruce Vawter, *Biblical Inspiration* (Philadelphia: Westminster, 1972), 71–72.

a variety of kinds of causation to account for the various cause-and-effect relationships he observed in the world.

Of the various categories of causality that Aristotle recognized, the Scholastics found the categories of *instrumental efficient* cause and *principal efficient* cause most useful. A familiar example of these types of causation is a person writing with a piece of chalk. The chalk is the instrumental efficient cause, since the writing depends on its potentialities to make a mark on a blackboard. Yet of itself the chalk is powerless to write. It needs the person to use it, who then functions as principal efficient cause, making use of the potential of the chalk and allowing it to perform its functions.[5]

That kind of thinking was then applied to understanding the way the Bible came into existence. God, the principal efficient cause, so motivated and inspired the biblical author, the instrumental efficient cause, that the author's potential for writing intelligible language was used for purposes, and to write materials, which the author alone could not have done. In that way, one could account for writings that had obviously been written by human beings, yet that would say more than human beings by themselves could have conceived or composed. The analogy had the additional advantage that it would enable one to account for Scripture coming ultimately from God yet being written in thoroughly human thought categories. God moves as principal efficient cause in such a way that the human potential and faculties of the author are in no way subverted or destroyed.[6] Such "inspiration," so it was argued, does not cancel human potentiality so much as it raises it. In that way human potentiality becomes capable of more than it could realize if left to its own devices.

This way of understanding the inspiration of Scripture can also account for the variety of literary styles and the multitude of literary forms found within the pages of inspired Scripture. If God's efficient causation enhances rather than suppresses the human potential, then

---

[5] I have drawn this information, along with much else, from the excellent book by Bruce Vawter.

[6] This method is a favorite of more conservative theologians, as for example B. B. Warfield, who argued God shaped the personality of the writer to produce precisely the divine message (*The Inspiration and Authority of the Bible*), quoted in Richard D. Land, "A Conservative Response" (Charles R. Blaisdell, ed., *Conservative, Moderate, Liberal* [St. Louis, Mo.: CBP Press, 1990]), 74.

all the natural idiosyncrasies of language and style of a given author, and all the literary conventions of a given time, would naturally appear in Scripture. It simply indicates that God, when he inspires, does not destroy the human element in his instrumental efficient cause.

Implicit in the idea of God as the principal efficient cause of Scripture, and in the attempts to account for the differing quality of portions of the Bible, is the conviction that the divine inspiration of the biblical authors occurs through the agency of the Holy Spirit. Here a distinction has been drawn between the *external* inspiration of the Spirit, and the *internal testimony* of that same Spirit. The latter term, to which we will need to return at a later point, refers to the gift of the Holy Spirit to the reader of Scripture. It is by that gift that the reader is enabled to believe that what is written in Scripture does in fact come from God and is therefore indispensable for salvation. Contrasted to that is the external inspiration of Scripture, by which is meant the fact that the authors wrote the words in the Bible under the power and authority of God working through his Spirit upon those authors. This activity of the Spirit became an issue at the time of the Reformation, and both the Reformers and the Roman Catholic Church affirmed that the Bible had been written by the agency of God's Spirit. Luther held that the authors had been the "channel" or the "tongue" of the Spirit, and Calvin liked to quote Isaiah 59:21, with its reference to "My spirit which rests on you and my words which I have put in your mouth" (NEB), when he spoke of the inspiration of Scripture.[7] The First Vatican Council declared that the biblical books have God as their author because they were written "under the inspiration of the Holy Spirit,"[8] and that view was confirmed in the Second Vatican Council, which also declared that all parts of the Bible, Old and New Testaments, were "committed to writing under the inspiration of the Holy Spirit."[9]

All of that makes it obvious why this way of understanding the inspiration of the Bible was used so frequently in the church from the Middle Ages right down to the present time. It allows one to affirm the human aspects of Scripture, which are evident to anyone who reads it, while at the same time allowing one to affirm that the

---

[7] This is discussed in Vawter, *Biblical Inspiration,* 65 (Luther) and 42 (Calvin).

[8] Ibid., 70.

[9] *Constitution on Divine Revelation,* ch. 3, "The Divine Inspiration and the Interpretation of Sacred Scripture," par. 11; cf. also pars. 7 and 9.

ultimate impulse for its composition lay not in the mind or intention of the author, but in God, who employed the various authors to accomplish his purpose of causing a Holy Scripture to be written.[10]

All of this is not to say that such a solution resolves every problem associated with trying to understand the way our Scriptures have been inspired. One example of such an unresolved problem lies in the obviously differing quality of the content of the various books of the Bible. Even a rapid reading of, say, Romans and the Song of Songs will show immediately that the former is far more useful for the Christian faith, or even for religious life in general, than the latter. The same would hold true for, say, the Gospel of Matthew or the Gospel of John, and portions of the book of Numbers or the epistle of Jude. How is one to account for such obvious variations in the quality of material inspired by God and contained in Scripture? One can, of course, solve the problem by denying that it exists, i.e., by insisting that the person who notes differing qualities simply shows in that way that he or she is incapable of finding the true message in those portions of Scripture identified as being of lesser quality. For those for whom such a solution is not acceptable, the only other alternative lies in accounting for those differences. One way is to speak of varying levels of inspiration. Thus James Orr, for example, can argue that while in some places the level of inspiration is at a "maximum," in other places it is operating on a "lower plane" with "feebler energy."[11] Such a notion is as old as the third century and the church father Origen, who, in an effort to resolve the tensions between the Gospels, thought that in the Gospels the authors wrote inspired material but also expressed their own opinions. Origen thought himself capable of differentiating between the divine and the human elements in both epistles and Gospels, and could even point to places where he felt the biblical authors,

---

[10] This analogy was by no means limited to the Scholastics of the medieval period. It also became the favorite analogy, although not so identified, of conservative Protestants in the English-speaking world; see A. A. Hodge and B. B. Warfield, "Inspiration," *The Presbyterian Review* 2 (1881): 225–60; Orr, *Revelation and Inspiration,* 169–70, as examples.

[11] Orr, *Revelation and Inspiration,* 177–78. William J. Abraham (*The Divine Inspiration of Holy Scripture* [Oxford: Oxford University Press, 1981], 63) makes the same point, although his method of first defining what inspiration means on a human level, and then applying it to God's activity with Scripture, is questionable at best. It assumes possible human meanings describe divine reality.

writing their own opinions, could have made mistakes.[12] The same view also surfaced at the time of the Reformation, when Erasmus sought to limit inspiration to those passages of Scripture which dealt with faith or morals. Some Roman Catholic scholars, writing in opposition to the Reformers and their followers, argued for differing kinds of inspiration in matters of prophecy on the one hand and history on the other. In the former instance the content itself was revealed, while in the matter of history, inspiration simply provided the impulse to record the events, perhaps also protecting the author from any errors.[13] Reformed orthodoxy formulated a similar view in its doctrine of the perspicuity of Scripture, by which the adherents meant that what is essential to salvation is clear in the Bible, even though other passages may remain puzzling or obscure. Thus, all things necessary for salvation in Scripture may be said to be of divine origin in a way that other, more obscure materials in Scripture were not.[14]

While this problem and others like it continue to evade a solution satisfactory to all those who want to understand Scripture as inspired, the difficulties have not had sufficient force to call into question the broad solution that God is the author of Scripture as principal efficient cause, inspiring by the Holy Spirit the authors of the various biblical books to write down what God wanted to have written down. This solution, though not always expressed in terms of "principal efficient cause," has maintained itself long after the influence of Aristotle waned, and, indeed, is widely accepted among people who are not even aware that such a way of understanding has anything to do with that Greek philosopher in the first place. The reason for the longevity of that solution lies in the fact that there is a close analogy to such an understanding of inspiration in the biblical figure of the prophet. That is, the Aristotelian idea of principal efficient cause found its best analogy and chief model in the biblical concept of "prophet," and it is in that form that this way of understanding inspiration has dominated theological reflections on the nature of inspiration to the virtual exclusion of all other forms.

---

[12] Cited and discussed in Vawter, *Biblical Inspiration,* 26.

[13] A good survey of this material can be found in ibid., 65–68, 134–36.

[14] See Heinrich Heppe, *Die Theologie der evangelisch-reformierten Kirche* (Neukirchen: Buchhandlung des Erziehungsvereins, 1958), 12–13.

INSPIRED AUTHORS

Because this has been such a key concept in Christian reflections on the way the Bible has been inspired, we must look carefully at the way the prophet functioned in the ancient world, both Jewish and Greek, and at the way those ancient cultural concepts functioned in the biblical idea of prophet and prophecy. Such an inquiry will give us a clearer idea of how the prophet was understood to function in his own context by his own contemporaries and how this analogy has been able to function for us as a model of the way in which Scriptures are inspired by God.

While the Old Testament idea of God inspiring his prophets is familiar enough to Christian readers, the fact that the ancient Greeks also had a concept of divinely inspired men and women may not be so familiar. We must have some grasp of it, however, not only to see how it differed from, but also to see in what ways it was similar to, early Hebraic thinking about the way God inspires human beings.

The ancient Greeks were conscious of the fact that poets and philosophers possessed gifts denied to ordinary men and women, and they accounted for these gifts by claiming that such people were inspired by the nine Muses, who gave songs to poets and divine thoughts to philosophers. In the process of such "inspiration" the normal rational powers of a human being were superseded, and the person was no longer in control of himself. Hence, the one into whom the divine Spirit was infused spoke or acted as a "divine man" and from a consciousness or volition other than his normal state of being.[15] It was from this vocabulary that the Septuagint, the Greek translation of the Old Testament, took the word *prophets* to translate the Hebrew word *nabi* to designate those whom God inspired or even possessed.

It is clear, however, that in the classical period of Hebrew prophecy the prophet was understood as a spokesman for God, but not in such a state that he was devoid of his own powers of reason and emotion. If the prophet spoke for God, and was granted visions and

---

[15] Vawter, *Biblical Inspiration,* 8–15 has a brief discussion and further references. See also Dewey M. Beegle, *Scripture, Tradition, and Infallibility* (Grand Rapids: Eerdmans, 1973), 127, and Robert Gnuse, *The Authority of the Bible: Theories of Inspiration, Revelation and the Canon of Scripture* (New York: Paulist Press, 1985), 17.

heard words of commission and of proclamation, he also entered into dialogue with God, thus clearly showing that even under inspiration the prophet remained conscious and in full possession of his or her own powers (see Exod. 3:1 to 4:17; Jer. 20:7–18).

It is precisely because the prophet is the one into whose mouth God has placed his own words, without thereby destroying the prophet as a human being, that the prophet became the model for an understanding of the inspiration of Scripture. Of all the prophets, Jeremiah is perhaps the clearest example of the usefulness of the prophetic model for inspiration. The words that Jeremiah has to speak to Israel were put into his mouth by God himself (Jer. 1:9; 2:1), but even more, Jeremiah at one point is commanded to write down the words that God had dictated to him (36:1–4, 32). Here, clearly, is a model that meets the test of inspiration: words written by human hands whose ultimate source is God. This way of understanding the inspiration of Scripture was then applied to the other books of the Bible and to other literary forms: poems, songs, histories, wisdom sayings, and all the rest. Behind the books of the Bible stand the inspired authors, each of whom wrote down what God wanted to be written down.[16] Such an understanding gives further impetus to the concept that it is the author, not the words he or she writes, that is inspired. Whether spoken or written, the language derives its inspiration from the prophetic person who speaks under divine inspiration, or who writes under the same impulse.

There is another element in Hebrew prophecy, however, which indicates that the prophet was not always in command of himself at the point of prophecy. The opening chapters of Ezekiel, for example (Ezek. 1:1 to 3:15), bear evidence of the reception of visions not understood and of receiving a message that is not communicated through hearing and understanding (2:9 to 3:3; Ezekiel "eats" the scroll with the message he is to speak). This idea of prophecy, familiar on the basis of our discussion of the Greek idea of "possession" by a divine Spirit, also has its roots deep in Israelite history. Driven by forces beyond their control, those early prophets were able to foretell the future, perform acts of clairvoyance, and carry out acts of physical endurance beyond

---

[16] So for example Jack W. Cottrell, "The Nature of Biblical Authority: A Conservative Perspective" (Charles R. Blaisdell, ed., *Conservative, Moderate, Liberal* [St. Louis, Mo.: CBP Press, 1990]), 28, 29.

the capacity of normal human beings (e.g., 1 Sam. 10:5–6, 10–13; 19:23–24; 1 Kgs. 18:12, 46; 2 Kgs. 2:16).[17]

It was this model of prophecy, in which the prophetic individual was totally possessed by an alien, albeit divine, force, that was taken over by both Jewish and early Christian scholars as the best way to understand the inspiration of sacred Scripture. Philo attributed prophecy to divine possession and compared inspiration to the surrender of a citadel that was then occupied by another power.[18] The early Christian writer Justin Martyr similarly seems to have understood inspiration in terms of a kind of mechanical dictation, on the analogy to his view of prophecy as a total possession by an outside force, in this case the Spirit of God.[19] Athenagoras, another early Christian author, similarly understood prophecy as an "ecstasy above the natural operations,"[20] and other early fathers, on the analogy of similar views of prophecy, understood the authors of Scripture to be "divine tools" in whom prophecy functioned to make the prophetic individual little more than a musical pick manipulated by the Spirit.[21]

Such an understanding of prophecy, and of the prophet as the model for understanding the inspiration of Scripture, continued its influence in the church through the Middle Ages and into the period of the Reformation. The view hardened in the subsequent period of Protestant orthodoxy: those books written by a prophet or an apostle were canonical, while all others were not.[22]

---

[17] For further discussion, see C. H. Dodd, *The Authority of the Bible* (London: James Nisbet & Co., 1948), 48–53, and see Vawter, *Biblical Inspiration*, 8–15 for a brief discussion and further references.

[18] So Reid, *The Authority of Scripture*, 168; see also Vawter, *Biblical Inspiration*, 14.

[19] So Markus Barth, *Conversation with the Bible* (New York: Holt, Rinehart & Winston, 1964), 108; Vawter, *Biblical Inspiration*, 14, 25. Beegle, *Scripture, Tradition, and Infallibility*, 132, argues against such a view on the part of Justin, but I think unsuccessfully.

[20] See Beegle, *Scripture, Tradition, and Infallibility*, 133; Vawter, *Biblical Inspiration*, 14, notes Athenagoras also compared the action of the Holy Spirit on the prophet to a piper blowing a flute.

[21] See Vawter, *Biblical Inspiration*, 25: Ignatius, the early Christian bishop of Antioch, attributed his own arguments for monarchial episcopal authority to a similar ecstatic possession by the Spirit, in his letter to the *Philadelphians* 7:1–2. I owe this reference to Dodd, *The Authority of the Bible*, 62.

[22] For a discussion of the scholastic period, see Vawter, *Biblical Inspiration*, 54–58; for Reformed orthodoxy, see Heppe, *Die Theologie der evangelisch-reformierten Kirche*, 10.

This view of inspiration continues to dominate the thinking of the conservative Christian scholars of our time, and is probably also the model assumed by most people who are untrained in theology. It is, to be sure, a simple and useful way to conceive of inspiration: God inspired the author of a given book in the Bible to write down what God wanted written.[23] Modern analyses of the nature of Scripture do make this view difficult to hold with respect to the way those books came into existence, and we must return to that problem in due course. Nevertheless, the prophetic model continues to hold sway in the thinking of many people about inspiration, even when they are not conscious that such thinking has been modeled on the picture of the Old Testament prophet.

The understanding of inspiration on the analogy of prophecy has had a further implication which has played a dramatic part in the discussions about the nature of the Bible in the late nineteenth and twentieth centuries. That implication concerns the kind of literature the inspired biblical authors produced. In its final form, as we shall see, that implication brought about the shift in the locus of inspiration from the person to the written words. That form of understanding inspiration has been designated by the term *plenary* or *plenary verbal* inspiration.

INSPIRED CONTENT

In its simplest form, such a view of inspiration asserts that God so guided the writers of Scripture by his Holy Spirit that they were incapable of writing anything contrary to his will, or even of writing anything that in any way could be considered untrue.[24] In sum, the words in Scripture are the words that God, not a human being, has

---

[23] So, for example, W. A. Criswell: "Everywhere in the Bible we find God speaking. It is God's voice, not man's" (quoted in Donald Bloesch, *Holy Scripture: Revelation, Inspiration, and Interpretation* in series *Christian Foundations* [Downers Grove, Ill.: InterVarsity, 1994], 95). A more sophisticated approach to inspiration which nevertheless retains the basic image of the prophet, i.e. the inspired individual, is that of Abraham, *Divine Inspiration*; see esp. 63–65.

[24] See Harold Lindsell, *The Battle for the Bible* (Grand Rapids: Zondervan, 1976), 33, for a current use of such a definition; see Beegle, *Scripture, Tradition, and Infallibility*, 145–46, for a quotation from and discussion of B. B. Warfield's classic definition.

chosen. This view of inspiration is by no means a modern invention. Philo, a Jewish scholar whose birth predated the Christian era, retold a story that a similar kind of inspiration had attended the translation of the Old Testament from Hebrew into Greek (the Septuagint). The inspiration of the translation was proved by the discovery that, although the translators worked independently of one another, their work was found to agree word for word, as though, Philo said, "dictated to each by an invisible prompter."[25] In a similar vein, the *Book of Jubilees* tells how Moses wrote the material in Genesis 1 to Exodus 12 at the dictation of the "angel of the presence," all in accordance with the direct command of God.[26] Thus, the very words themselves come from God.

Such language about the way Scripture was inspired is also found in the early period of the church. The idea, for example, that prophets under divine inspiration could utter things they themselves did not fully comprehend, would lend itself to the understanding that they were simply recording the words God dictated directly to them.[27] Although this language was present in that period, however, it did not represent the dominant view. Nor did the idea of inspiration as the transcription of God's own dictated words occupy a central position during the Scholastic period, although, again, there are allusions to it. It was not until the period of Protestant orthodoxy that the concept of divine, verbal dictation came to be the dominant way scriptural inspiration was understood. During that period, beginning in the late seventeenth century, a kind of consensus did emerge that inspiration meant that the Holy Spirit had verbally dictated Scripture to its respective authors.[28] One theologian of that period went so far as to conclude that since the Bible had enjoyed such an origin, it would not rightly be considered a creature.[29] The confession that was formulated by the Swiss Reformed Church (*Formula Consensus Helvetica*) affirmed that not only the words but the very letters were inspired.[30]

---

[25] *Life of Moses,* 2.31–37; the quotation is from par. 37.

[26] The *Book of Jubilees,* chs. 1, 2. The tradition here may be drawing on the imagery of Exod. 24:12. For similar language about the Torah in the Talmud, see the discussion in Beegle, *Scripture, Tradition, and Infallibility,* 130–31.

[27] For a discussion of the use of such language by the later Scholastics, see Vawter, *Biblical Inspiration,* 60–62; on Aquinas, 55.

[28] See Reid, *Authority of Scripture,* 84–86.

[29] Vawter, *Biblical Inspiration,* 81.

[30] Ibid., 82.

That kind of view of the inspiration of the Bible tends, however, to raise again questions having to do with the literary style of the Bible. If the Holy Spirit dictated every word, how can one account for differences in style and vocabulary? Above all, how can one account for infelicities of style and grammar? Can God be the source of anything imperfect? That problem also occurred to some early Christian thinkers in their reflections about the Holy Scripture, and they concluded that such diversities were part of the deliberate strategy of God in producing Scripture. They termed this strategy *condescension* or *accommodation.* Dating as early as the time of John Chrysostom, the concept of accommodation simply asserts that since Scriptures were intended to be understood at a particular place and time, with specific intellectual potential and accomplishments, God accommodated his message to the language, thought forms, and modes of expression that would be readily comprehensible. Thus, Scriptures written in different times will be cast in different forms, in each instance, however, in forms understandable to the time when they were produced. In that way, scholars sought, and in some cases still seek, to account for the time-conditioned nature in which those truths were cloaked.[31] If, as such an understanding of Scripture tends to assume, the Bible contains timeless truths, this is one way to account for the time-conditioned form in which those truths were cloaked.[32]

A further implication of the idea that God dictated Scripture through the inspiration of his Holy Spirit appears in the assertion that since God is not false, every word in Scripture must be true. This idea that Scripture is free from all error, whether concerning history, biology, geology, or doctrine, is usually termed *inerrancy* and seeks to defend the Bible against any charge that it contains error of any kind. How could it, if God in fact has, at least figuratively, dictated every word through his Holy Spirit? There are a number of problems with such a defense of the content of the Bible, and it has not, contrary to the assertions of some of its defenders, been the dominant view in the

---

[31] For a good discussion of *accommodation,* see ibid., the section beginning on p. 40; see also pp. 60–61.

[32] Some critics have compared such a view of the Bible to the heresy that Christ's human nature was merely appearance, not reality, a view called *docetism;* cf. G. C. Berkouwer, *Holy Scripture: Studies in Dogmatics* (Grand Rapids: Eerdmans, 1975), 18.

history of the church.[33] There is also the problem of defining *error*. Does it mean a willful untruth on the part of the author? Does it mean a mistake in biology or geology? How can it be squared with the idea of accommodation, in which God spoke in a time-conditioned way, a way our age no longer believes represents scientific truth? For that reason there has arisen a conflict among conservative Christians as to whether the term *inerrancy* is the most useful way to describe what they want to affirm.[34] However such questions be resolved—and again we will want to return to a discussion of them in another context—for many people, inspiration has come to be equated with inerrancy in the most wooden understanding of that term: no mistakes of any sort in any part of the Bible, based on what we as twentieth-century people of Western culture now think to be true.[35] We shall return in the next chapter to a more complete discussion of this way of understanding the inspiration of Scripture.

IMPACT ON OTHER THEOLOGICAL PROBLEMS

As we noted at the beginning of this chapter, not only has the understanding of inspiration taken on a wide variety of forms, as theologians sought to find a way to express convictions about the mode of inspiration and the nature of Scripture, but the way in which inspiration is understood has clear implications for the way further theological problems are resolved. We will illustrate such implications by means of four examples: the effect of inspiration on the certainty of faith, on the way the authority of Scripture is understood, on the way

---

[33] Again, see the discussion in Vawter, *Biblical Inspiration*, the section beginning on p. 132. This view tends to crop up when the authority of the Bible is perceived to be under attack, as in the period of Protestant orthodoxy, on which see Heppe, *Die Theologie der evangelisch-reformierten Kirche*, 11–12.

[34] For an example, see *Biblical Authority*, ed. by Jack Rogers (Waco: Word Books, 1977), 178–79; Davis, *Debate About the Bible*, ch. 6, beginning on p. 114.

[35] One difficulty with inerrancy of the Bible in scientific matters is that scientific *truth*, i.e., statements about *the way things are objectively*, tends to change from time to time. Can the Bible be *inerrant* for its contemporary readers in the time of *both* pre-Galilean *and* post-Galilean astronomy? Or was the Bible written to be inerrant only for late twentieth-century Western civilization? We will return to this question below.

the unity of the Bible is expressed, and on the relationship between the Bible and revelation.

The question of the certainty of faith makes it clear that more than theoretical reflections are involved in the way one understands the inspiration of Scripture. One of the questions that defenders of the view of inerrancy like to ask their opponents is: "If the Bible is not true in all its parts, how can you be sure it is true in any of its parts?" That is, if some parts are open to doubt, how can one have any certainty about the credibility of any part? Perhaps the part most needed for our faith is also in error. What then becomes of the certainty of faith?[36] If the Bible is wrong on historical or botanical matters, how can one be sure it is not also wrong in matters necessary to faith, such as the fact that Jesus was God incarnate or that he rose from the dead? With questions such as these, defenders of the view of the inerrancy of Scripture seek to establish the certainty of faith and to call into question the possibility of similar certainty for those who do not share that view of the mode of inspiration.

People who do not regard inerrancy as a valid mode of understanding inspiration, however, will point out that the reasoning which equated certainty with the view of inerrancy is beset with serious problems, principally because the kind of certainty that it desires in religious and historical matters is simply not available outside the realm of logic and mathematics.[37] A further problem consists in the fact that such *knowledge* in matters of our sin and our divine forgiveness through Christ is simply not available, if knowledge be defined as something that we know from publicly verifiable evidence and that is thus immune from doubt. Critics of such a view point out that *knowledge* is here being confused with *faith,* since faith alone is the appropriate stance in the face of our sin and God's merciful forgiveness of it. Such faith cannot be based on a theoretical reflection (inerrancy) that seeks to impose a prior category on revelation and its biblical witness if it is to be accepted as trustworthy.[38] Such critics also point out that people

---

[36] This point was made recently in a statement from the 1978 meeting of the International Council on Biblical Inerrancy, held in Chicago.

[37] A good discussion of this whole problem can be found in Davis, *Debate About the Bible,* 68–77. He points to the origin of such a view of knowledge in the thinking of Descartes, the French philosopher.

[38] See Berkouwer, *Holy Scripture,* 30–33, on this point.

do not operate in other areas of life on the principle that one mistake or error renders all other statements or acts coming from that source totally untrustworthy. One's trust in a friend is not irrevocably shattered if one finds that in some matter of historical information that friend should prove to be in error. Life has a way of continuing to function even in the absence of absolute certainty, and whatever else the Bible may concern, it is surely about life. Since life is what Scripture is all about, it would be foolish to expect from Scripture a kind of lifeless certainty in matters of sin and salvation. Those who hold that inspiration of Scripture does not imply its inerrancy thus point to the content of Scripture which inspires trust in a living God as the basis for certainty in faith. The view one takes of inspiration will thus have a strong influence on how one defines certainty of faith, and where one looks in Scripture to find it.

If the certainty of faith is bound up, for good or ill, with the view one takes about the nature of inspiration, a second aspect of faith also connected to it is the matter of the authority of Scripture. Obviously, if the Bible does not have its origins in some unique way in the will of God, if it is a book like any other book, then no more authority can be claimed for it than for any other book. The nature and locus of inspiration, in short, will determine the authority that we may claim for Scripture. Whatever authority Scripture will have, therefore, will depend on its relationship to God. Some have sought to define that relationship in terms of the use God makes of Scripture to awaken faith and obedience in those who hear its message. The Bible's authority will then lie not so much in the accuracy of its historical reporting or on its ability to anticipate discoveries of modern sciences. Rather, its authority will lie in the way in which it brings to bear in the contemporary world the significance of the events and people about which it speaks. It will be authoritative as an instrument in accomplishing God's plan of salvation, bearing witness to God's will and to the way he has accomplished his purposes in the past.[39] Others will want to affirm, however, that unless the authority of the Scripture can

---

[39] Good discussions of this view can be found in James Barr, *The Bible in the Modern World* (London: SCM, 1973), beginning on p. 23, and in Barth, *Conversation with the Bible*, in the chapter entitled "The Authority of a Charter of Liberty." Barth remarks that in viewing the Bible as God's instrument to make known his will one must not confuse the tool with the one who uses it, p. 187.

be based on the objectifiable truth contained in Scripture, that authority will be far too subjective in nature to be significant. Unless the
authority of Scripture can be an external, objective authority, it will
rest too much in the consciousness of the one who reads it, and thus
must ultimately be considered too subjective.[40] How we understand
inspiration, therefore, will be closely related to the way in which we
understand the mode and function of the authority of Scripture.[41]

A further issue, intimately related to the question of the inspiration of Scripture, is the question of the unity of the Bible. Some
have sought to solve this question again on the basis of a prior
assumption, namely, that if God is the author through inspiration of
all Scripture, then Scripture will be a unity because it has but one
author. This will be reinforced if one holds that all parts of Scripture
are equally inspired, in which case that unitary inspiration will be
applicable to all parts of the Bible, and hence, on this prior assumption, all parts will bear the marks of one unified whole.[42] It then
becomes the task of the interpreter to find this unity and to explain—or explain away—any parts of Scripture that do not seem to
share that unity. It is just at the point of needing to demonstrate from
Scripture itself the validity of the prior assumption about its unity
that difficulties arise, however. Just as the more conservative view of
inspiration faces a major problem in demonstrating its contention
that there are no errors of fact in Scripture, so it faces a major
problem in attempting to eliminate discrepancies, not to say contradictions, that appear within the pages of the Bible. The classical way
of finding unity has been the allegorical method, by which a text may
be found to say something other than its more obvious meaning. In
any case, a view of inspiration that must posit a consistency of
viewpoint throughout Scripture will be severely challenged by any
difficulty in demonstrating that consistency passage-by-passage. Any
view of inspiration must be able either to explain or to explain away

---

[40] This position developed significantly in the period of Protestant orthodoxy,
which sought an objective ground of faith beyond that which either Luther or
Calvin had found necessary; see Reid, *Authority of Scripture,* esp. 92, 100.

[41] We will return to the understanding of the authority of the Bible in our final
chapter.

[42] See James Barr, *Fundamentalism* (Philadelphia: Westminster, 1978), 65; Hodge and
Warfield, "Inspiration," 226.

evidences that would argue against a single, unified theological viewpoint in Scripture. The definition of *unity* will also be significant here, namely, whether unity in doctrine or theology be conceived in a broader or narrower sense. If a narrower sense faces the problem of apparent disunity in Scripture, a broader sense faces the problem of being so broad that any real meaning to unity is lost. However one may define unity, though, one's view of the nature of inspiration will affect what one is able to affirm about the coherence of viewpoint represented in the Bible.

Still another theological issue closely tied up with the way in which inspiration of Scripture is understood concerns the relationship between the Bible and revelation. Those who understand the nature of revelation to be of such kind that it is found in those acts of God by which he sets forth his plan of salvation for humankind, i.e., in the exodus of Israel from Egypt or the career, death, and resurrection of Jesus, will also find the locus of inspiration in those events and will then understand the Bible as the record of such events, and hence as the record of revelation. If God reveals himself in history, indeed in particular events within human history, then the Bible, in identifying those revelatory events, will be a record of those events. In that case, the Bible is the *witness* to God's revelation of himself as righteous savior.[43] Yet, as the Bible itself indicates, those events are capable of being misunderstood and misinterpreted (e.g., false prophets, Pharisaic rejection of Jesus). Can we, some ask, rely on revelation if its understanding is so fragile that it is open to many differing interpretations? If God wanted to reveal himself, would he not do it in a less ambiguous way, especially if our salvation is in some way intimately related to that revelation? In that case, the revelation must be sought not in the events but in the correct interpretation of those events, i.e., in the Bible itself. If one believes that the inspiration of the Bible is directly from God, and includes the words of Scripture themselves, then the locus of revelation will obviously be those words. In that case, the Bible is not the record of or witness to revelation, it is itself revelation. God reveals himself to us in the theological truths re-

---

[43] Good discussions of this kind of view can be found in Orr, *Revelation and Inspiration,* 156–59; Barth, *Conversation with the Bible,* esp. 138–39; Berkouwer, *Holy Scripture,* 165–69. This view was characteristic of the theological movement known as "Neo-orthodoxy."

corded by the divinely inspired authors.[44] How one understands inspiration, therefore, and how one understands revelation, will closely affect each other, and changes in the one will inevitably bring about changes in the other.

We have now concluded our rapid survey of some of the problems associated with an attempt to formulate an understanding of the inspiration of Scripture, and we have seen how that formulation affects, and is affected by, some other theological problems. Such a survey has indicated the areas within which we move when we approach the problem of the inspiration of the Bible, and it will equip us to understand some of the problems and the issues which are debated among those who hold differing opinions on the nature of that inspiration. We want, therefore, as our next step, to survey two such attempts to formulate an understanding of the nature of scriptural inspiration, attempts which we will call, for lack of better terminology, liberal and conservative.[45]

---

[44] This view is frequently characterized with the catchword *propositional revelation.* It is characteristic of the movement known as Fundamentalism.

[45] These are notoriously slippery and indefinite terms. Their meaning is virtually always determined by the theological stance of the one who uses them, and hence they are quite relative. *Liberal* in this context will be applied to those who use it as a self-designation, and *conservative* will be applied to those who use such self-designations as *evangelicals* or *Bible-believing Christians.*

Two Contemporary
Views Considered

What we shall attempt in the following pages is by no means an exhaustive exposition of the two contrasting alternatives for viewing the nature of Scripture and for understanding its inspiration and authority. Nor can we take account of the various nuances that characterize individual viewpoints within the large rubrics of *liberal* and *conservative*. Rather, our task will be to outline some of the major characteristics of these two views, characteristics which to some degree at least are agreed upon by most of the proponents of the respective views; then we will evaluate some of the problems that remain unresolved. Such an approach by no means intends to imply that these are the only alternatives available to modern Christians or that our sketch represents the only configuration the alternatives can take. Our intention is simply to look at two contemporary ways of understanding the nature of Scripture, its inspiration and authority, in order to see how some of the problems outlined above find their place within a larger theological perspective.

THE LIBERAL VIEW

What we shall term the *liberal* view is characteristically impressed with the nature of Scripture, and expositions of our problem frequently begin with a description of the phenomena in the Bible that point to the nature and origins of that collection of writings. Among the phenomena to which these authors point are, for example, the

contradictions that they find in the Bible. For example, in Deuteronomy 10:1–5, Moses follows God's command that he build the ark of
the covenant, while in Exodus 37:1–9, Bezalel is its artificer. In Acts 9:7,
Paul's companions heard the voice but saw nothing, while in Acts 22:9,
they saw the light but heard nothing. The two accounts of the manner
of Judas' death and the naming of the Field of Blood in Acts 1:16–19
and Matthew 27:3–10 are found to be in sharp contradiction, and any
attempt to work out an accurate account of the sequence of events
following Jesus' resurrection will find contradictory evidence in one
or more of the Gospel accounts.[1] A survey of the whole Bible will
reveal, by similar evidence, that the various authors were prone to
mistakes both of detail and of religious significance in the events they
describe.[2] Again, argue liberal proponents, the biblical narratives betray the same kind of "prescientific" materials that one finds in the
ancient literatures of other peoples and countries, such as the stories
that tell about how certain animals acquired their present forms and
habits (e.g., Gen. 3:14–15), the great ages achieved by heroes of earlier
times (e.g., Gen. 5), and other tales which were freely embellished by
the imaginations of the persons who first told them.[3] Similar to such
prescientific materials are what are termed "contradictions of known
truth," such as the effect of visual stimuli on reproducing animals
(Jacob increased both the quantity and quality of his flocks by letting
the breeding animals view striped sticks, Gen. 30:35–43), the possibility
of stopping the sun in its path as it moved around the earth (Josh.
10:12–15), and the explanation of disease as demonic possession.[4] In
addition, liberal scholars affirm, there are passages in which morally
questionable, if not unworthy, acts and sentiments are recorded (e.g.,
Ps. 18:20–24, 33–49; 109).[5]

What all of this means is that the Scriptures have been condi-
tioned by the culture within which they originated in the same way

---

[1] I have taken this sampling from L. Harold DeWolf, *A Theology of the Living Church*
(rev. ed.; New York: Harper & Brothers, 1960), 68–69. (Hereafter cited as *A Theology*.)

[2] See L. Harold DeWolf, *The Case for Theology in Liberal Perspective* (Philadelphia:
Westminster, 1959), 47–48. (Hereafter cited as *The Case*.)

[3] DeWolf, *A Theology*, 71–72.

[4] Examples drawn from DeWolf, *A Theology*, 71.

[5] These examples were again selected from those cited by DeWolf, *A Theology*,
72–73.

that all other writings are so affected. If ancient Semites generally thought that firmament and earth formed a bubble suspended in the midst of endless water, so did the author of Genesis, who can account for the flood by observing that water burst forth up through the earth as well as coming down through the opened windows of the firmament above (Gen. 7:11). That also means that some of the materials in Scripture will be of more value to us than some others, depending on the extent to which they have been formulated in cultural terms we no longer think true.[6]

Although both broader types and specific examples of evidence given in various liberal accounts of the inspiration of Scripture could be multiplied, we have seen enough to understand the basis on which conclusions are drawn about the nature of Scripture. If the quality of the material differs and is uneven, then we must conclude that there are varying degrees of inspiration. If some writings show a maximum "divine element," others show it at a minimum.[7] If the level of truth in some writings is high, in others it is low.[8] All of that leads to the conclusion that one may not view the Bible as being of equal inspiration throughout. Rather than being in its totality the revelation of God, it is instead the human record of that revelation, carrying with it, as such a record, all the ills to which human accounts are heir.[9] As human understanding and spiritual sensitivity increased, the accounts of God's "mighty deeds" became correspondingly of higher quality and utility. Indeed as "men were prepared through progressive stages of understanding, obedience and humble spiritual sensitiveness," God could show "increasing measures of His truth to humanity."[10] Hence we find reflected in the literature of the Bible the same progressive understanding of truth that we find reflected in the whole history of humanity, as succeeding ages increased in knowledge and moral sensitivity. Scripture therefore must be seen as a collection of materials written by fallible human beings who reflected the culture out of

---

[6] See DeWolf, *The Case*, 52–55.

[7] Beegle, *Scripture, Tradition, and Infallibility*, 206–8; DeWolf, *A Theology*, 82–83.

[8] See DeWolf, *The Case*, 48; in *A Theology*, DeWolf shows that Irenaeus and Tertullian, early church fathers, implicitly acknowledged the same point by the way they used Scripture, p. 81.

[9] DeWolf, *A Theology*, 79.

[10] Ibid., 75.

which they came and for which they were writing. Accordingly, Scripture itself is best described as a mixture of the word of God with the erring words of its human authors.

All of this has implications for the way we must work out our view of the nature of the inspiration of the Bible, how we are to understand and use it, and the kind of authority we can ascribe to it. It will be useful to examine each of those areas in turn.

We have already seen that the liberal view must insist that the Bible contains material of differing value and quality, and that those materials bear the marks of the cultures out of which they emerged and for which they were written. Those are characteristics the Bible shares with any literature, ancient or modern. Because of those facts, a tendency emerged in some quarters in the late eighteenth and nineteenth centuries to see Scripture as on a par with all other ancient literature. Its origins had to be accounted for in the way one accounted for any other literature bearing the same characteristics, and that meant that, like other ancient literature, the Bible had only human origins.[11] The Bible then becomes simply one of the man-made sourcebooks of the Christian religion, and it becomes necessary to say only as much about the inspiration of the Bible as one would want to say about the inspiration of any other literature. That is, the quality of the various biblical books derives from the quality of their authors and their own inspiration as "religious geniuses."[12] Moved by a remarkable religious experience, the biblical writers set down the record of what they understood about the ways of God with humanity, a record that shares the grandeur and the shortcomings of any other piece of literature.[13]

Inspiration may therefore be defined in this way: "The Bible as a whole was accomplished by an extraordinary stimulation and elevation

---

[11] This was the view of Herder, Lessing, Ritschl, and Gunkel, among others; see Vawter, *Biblical Inspiration,* 89, 126.

[12] See Beegle, *Scripture, Tradition, and Infallibility,* 308–9; Reid, *The Authority of Scripture,* 167–69; such a view does enable one to account for the human errors that liberals find in the Bible.

[13] Reid, *The Authority of Scripture,* 167; on this basis, Barr has suggested that rather than calling the Bible the word of God, it would be more appropriate and more accurate to speak of it as the "Word of Israel" or the "Word of some leading early Christians" (*The Bible in the Modern World,* 120).

of the powers of men who devoutly yielded themselves to God's will, and sought, often with success unparalleled elsewhere, to convey truth useful to the salvation of men and of nations."[14] If the view that operates with such a definition was impressed with the phenomena of Scripture which linked it, in its primitive outlook and internal contradictions, with other similar literature, that same view is also impressed with the evidences that point to the high inspiration of this literature. The substance of thought which seems to defy human ability to express it adequately; the records of uniquely important events which led to spiritual victory despite, indeed through, tragedy; the passages that rise to lofty heights of spiritual beauty, rhetorical dignity, and power, which are able in the present, as they were able in the past, to inspire men and women to seek and find God—all of these point to the high, even unique degree of inspiration evident in the pages of Holy Scripture.[15]

There is no intention, therefore, in such a view to deny either the inspiration or the authority of Scripture. The aim is simply to conform the understanding of such inspiration and authority to the kind of literature the liberals are convinced the Bible represents.

This view of the nature of the Bible and the character of its inspiration also has implications for the way the Bible may be used within the Christian church. It is obvious that on this view of inspiration, the usefulness of every word in Scripture is by no means guaranteed. In a collection of literature of such uneven quality, not everything in the Bible is essential, or even useful, for salvation. The reader faces the task, therefore, of separating the kernel of divine wisdom from the husk of the human ideas in which it has been conveyed, once he or she has decided which portions of Scripture do in fact contain such divine wisdom. Since the words of Scripture are fully human and need critical evaluation, the reader must learn to discriminate between the word of God and the words of human beings, lest one think it as important to follow Paul's advice about long hair (1 Cor. 11:14) as to follow Jesus' command to love one's enemies (Matt. 5:44).[16]

---

[14] DeWolf, *A Theology*, 76.

[15] These examples were taken from DeWolf, *A Theology*, 77–80; they could easily be paralleled in other authors of this persuasion.

[16] This position is reflected in DeWolf, *A Theology*, 76; *The Case*, 49, 55, 57; Barr, *Fundamentalism*, 288.

At least two ways of evaluating biblical material are suggested by L. H. DeWolf, a notable proponent of the liberal view: one must compare and measure all else in the Bible by the teaching of Jesus, but above that, one must apply as criterion the "totality of human experience," secular as well as religious. On that basis, whatever we find in the Bible that is "contrary to our systematic, substantial knowledge, we recognize as part of the dated human error."[17] Whether this criterion be termed God's "general revelation," or "the sum total of human experience," it is clear that the reader of the Bible is to use his or her critical judgment in deciding what is acceptable as the word of God, and what is simply human words.[18]

Such a view also affects the way in which one understands the authority of the Bible. It is obvious that the highest authority in such a view is the sum total of human experience. One may therefore accept as authoritative only that material in the Bible that is confirmed by humanity's total experience, secular as well as sacred. That is, one must test historical, geological, botanical, and other such materials in the Bible in the light of our present knowledge of these sciences, and accept what conforms to such current knowledge. Similarly, one must test the moral and religious content of the Bible against the best of human experience in order to determine what may continue to have authority for us in our world. One would not, for example, want to attribute equal moral authority to the imprecatory psalms, or the "legends of the bloodthirsty heroes in the Judges," on the one hand, and to the sayings of Jesus on the others.[19] The Bible therefore can no longer represent an unquestioned authority. What does retain final authority is God himself, who speaks to us through many channels. Since he speaks supremely in Christ, and since the Bible is our primary source of knowledge about him, the Bible does retain high authority, but only within the larger context of God's communication with humanity through the totality of his creation and its history.[20]

---

[17] DeWolf, *The Case*, 36; see also his *A Theology*, 83–85.

[18] DeWolf, *The Case*, 56–57.

[19] The examples come from DeWolf, *A Theology*, 83.

[20] This represents a higher valuation on "general revelation" than more conservative scholars might be willing to give. In a sense, it established "general revelation" as a mode superior to "special revelation" in Israel and Christ. For other criticisms, see Barth, *Conversation with the Bible*, beginning with p. 137.

Christian certainty therefore does not lie in total and unquestioning acceptance of the witness of Scripture. Rather, it lies in the word made flesh in Jesus, a word which must be received with "reverence and a sense of personal dependence on God." All reading of the Bible must thus be accompanied by "earnest prayer."[21] Within this total context of the community that similarly values the Bible as the witness to Christ, however fallible that witness in its present form may be, the believer will find the authority of Scripture by which he or she may then, to be sure not uncritically, live out faith in the confidence that the ongoing work of the Spirit, present both within the Christian community and in the totality of experiences open to the human being, will continue to bear witness to the divine presence in the world.

STRENGTHS AND WEAKNESSES OF THE LIBERAL VIEW

Although the presentation of the conservative view will indicate clearly enough the areas in which criticism can and has been leveled against the liberal view of Scripture, we may single out one or two items that indicate both the strengths and the weaknesses of such a view. In the first instance, the liberal view does not find what we may term the negative phenomena of Scripture (i.e., internal contradictions, errors of fact) an embarrassment. The commands to slaughter all inhabitants of a captured Canaanite town (e.g., Josh. 6:17; 8:18–27), the vindictiveness of a psalmist (e.g., Ps. 137), the tensions and contradictions within various portions of Scripture, the assumptions about the world that contradict our own scientific knowledge—all of these can be understood as the words of fallible human beings of another culture who sought to express their understanding of the ways of God with humanity. Similarly, the fact that errors have crept in as Scripture was copied over and over do not present a problem for this view, since there is no claim that the text itself is in any way inerrant or infallible. The liberal need not appeal to an inerrant autograph.

Problems raised by the selection of the canon can also be satisfactorily solved for the liberal on this view of Scripture. Lack of an

---

[21] DeWolf, *A Theology*, 86; cf. idem, *The Case*, 53–54.

infallible text means that one need not worry about an infallible choice of books to be included in the canon. All can be understood within the normal parameters of human activity. Indeed, if the Bible is but one source of the total tradition of Israel and the church, one may gratefully learn from it what one can without the pressure of having to defend the assertions that the Bible contains only the best books from that tradition and that all traditions outside the boundaries of the canon are morally and spiritually inferior. Furthermore, one need not suspend one's ordinary critical faculties when reading this literature. It is to be understood, in all its cultural relatedness, in the same way that one understands, or seeks to understand, any ancient document.

On the other hand, the liberal view which we have just reviewed does dilute in a significant way the concepts of inspiration and authority in relation to Scripture. On the matter of inspiration, this view tends to localize it in the individual on the basis either of the supreme religious experience undergone by that person, or some inherent superiority generally called "religious genius." This raises two problems. The first leads one to wonder how this view can assign more spiritual authority to biblical books than to any other books written under the power of some great religious experience, or by someone equally possessed of such genius. Why should one prefer, say, Leviticus to Dante's *Inferno*, or Jude to Thomas à Kempis's *Imitation of Christ?* On such a view, one is hard put to give an answer, yet proponents of the liberal view of the Bible rarely suggest in any serious way that such later, or even earlier, writings be used in public worship in place of Holy Writ. The consequences of the theory, in this case, outrun the willingness of those who hold it to follow them to their conclusion. A further problem concerns the ability of ordinary people to understand one whom we term a "genius." The fruit of genius is often beyond the grasp of others less gifted. Again, what of the concept "revelation" if the one who writes Scripture is inherently a genius? Revelation would then lie in the genes of the author rather than in some divine communication.

A further difficulty lies in the idea of progressive revelation. This idea asserts that because—as humankind matured mentally and spiritually—later stages of divine revelation are superior to earlier ones, we may therefore usefully, indeed, are required to, judge the earlier in terms of the later. Again, there are two problems, one theoretical, one practical. Theoretically, such maturation and spiritual growth can hardly have stopped two thousand years ago. A person is thus driven to the same conclusion here as in relation to the notion of inspiration predicated on religious experience, namely, one ought logically to find more authority in spiritual writings composed after the New Testament period, since they would represent a further maturation of mental and spiritual power. Practically, that leads us to have to posit that somehow we are more spiritual than, say, a Moses or a Micah and are in a better position to understand the will of God than, say, a Paul or a Peter. Here, a Hegelian doctrine of continuing progress, discredited by the wars of the twentieth century, has continued its influence on religious thought. Changing cultures demand changing modes of expression, but our own recent history ought to have taught us not to equate our particular culture and its modes of expression with inherent moral superiority. Joshua is hardly a greater murderer than Hitler or Stalin or Pol Pot, on any scale of judgment. Ancient moral perversion is hardly more bizarre than Jonestown in Guyana.[22]

All of this indicates that, for the most part, those who have held the liberal view of Scripture have been unwilling to apply to their religious life the logical consequences of the doctrine of Scripture they have enunciated. That is of course not to condemn all insights achieved by means of this view of Scripture. We shall seek to make positive use of a number of them later on in our discussion. It is simply to point out why we are persuaded that such a view of Holy Scripture is not adequate for either public or private spiritual life.

If the liberal view tends to lose the Bible in the larger cultural context, the conservative view suffers from the necessity of isolating the Bible from that context. We must now turn to an exposition of that way of looking at the inspiration of Scripture.

THE CONSERVATIVE VIEW

If, as we saw, it is characteristic for the liberal view of Scripture to begin with the phenomena of the Bible and to formulate a doctrine

---

[22] There are of course many more criticisms of the liberal view of Scripture, especially from a more conservative viewpoint. A summary of such criticisms may conveniently be found in *The Foundation of Biblical Authority* (ed. by James M. Boice; Grand Rapids: Zondervan, 1978), beginning on p. 66.

of Scripture that then takes them into account, the conservative view reverses the order. This view is of course aware of such phenomena, but they play a secondary, not to say problematic, role for the conservative formulation of the nature of the inspiration of the Bible. Primary for the conservative view is the affirmation that the Bible has as its ultimate source God himself, and that because God cannot lie or contradict himself, the Bible cannot contain any errors or inconsistencies.[23] While there is some attention given to confirming such a view from Scripture itself, a point to which we will return, the real power of this view lies in that prior assumption. If the prior assumption of the actual inerrancy of Scripture were set aside, demonstrations of inerrancy from Scripture could as easily be dismissed as accepted. It is only the assumption that everything the Bible says is true that gives any force at all to a biblical witness concerning inerrancy. The liberal view, which does not share the presupposition of inerrancy, for example, is not convinced of such inerrancy by scriptural witness.

This view can also be stated in another way, namely, that unless one can affirm that Scripture is inerrant, one cannot affirm the veracity of God.[24] In a sense, virtually the entire range of conservative doctrinal formulations finally depends on this one fundamental statement: God is truth, God is the source of Scripture, and therefore Scripture must also be truth. If God, the author of Scripture, cannot lie, then neither can Scripture. The doctrine of Scripture is therefore the touchstone for all other doctrines within this conservative purview. We must now see how that works itself out in relation to the conservative

---

[23] See, for example, Boice, ed., *Foundation of Biblical Authority,* 15; Lindsell, *Battle for the Bible,* 182; *Summit Papers,* International Council on Biblical Inerrancy, ed. by Norman L. Geisler (Oakland, Calif.: ICBI, n.d.), p. 7.35; J. W. Cottrell, "The Nature of Biblical Authority," 29. Rogers, ed., *Biblical Authority,* 30–31, argues that one source for such a position that some reasonable proof (inerrancy of Scripture) must precede faith (its content is true) is derived from the Aristotelian-Thomistic method of putting reason before faith. This position was of utmost importance for the theologian Turretin, who was instrumental in the formulation of the Helvetic Consensus Formula of 1675, and who was highly influential among conservative Reformed theologians in this country, especially the Princeton theology of Hodge and Warfield. See also pp. 40–41; Barr, *Fundamentalism,* 276–77 on this point.

[24] See Geisler, ed., *Summit Papers,* 7.37 as an example.

understanding of the nature of inspiration, and the problems which, as we have seen, are related to that area of Christian doctrine.

As one might expect, for the conservative view, inspiration of Scripture carries to the very words themselves. Again and again, conservatives will insist that not only the thoughts conveyed by the words of the Bible but those very words themselves have been inspired by God through his Holy Spirit.[25] In this process, the conservatives recognize, God used the contemporary culture of his "penmen"[26] in his inspiration of them, so that what they wrote bears linguistic and cultural characteristics of the time in which it was written. Yet those "penmen" were not limited to the knowledge available to their age. Inspiration involves knowledge from both natural and supernatural sources.[27] More importantly, however, than the positive statement about the content of Scripture is the negative assertion that God, by his inspiration, moved the writers of Scripture in such a way as to prevent them from writing any errors. Inspiration therefore produced a document that is inerrant in all its statements.[28]

With that equation of inspiration and inerrancy, we have touched the nerve of the conservative view of Scripture. Such inerrancy means simply that the Bible is free from factual error in all its statements, down to the most minute and incidental details.[29] Such freedom from error is not limited to religious affirmations or statements pertaining to divine matters or to morality. It covers all statements of any kind made anywhere in the Bible.[30] To be sure, Scripture is not designed to teach science, history, or philosophy. Nevertheless, conservatives never tire of affirming that where statements of science, or history, or geog-

---

[25] For example, Hodge and Warfield, "Inspiration," 233, 234; *The Chicago Statement on Biblical Inerrancy* of the International Council on Biblical Inerrancy (hereafter cited as *Chicago Statement*), art. VI; cf. also Orr, *Revelation and Inspiration,* 209, although in important respects, he disavows the conservative position, especially on verbal inerrancy.

[26] This word is used in the *Chicago Statement* in its Exposition, "Infallibility, Inerrancy, Interpretation," par. 4. That cultural milieu was also under God's providence and control, however.

[27] So Hodge and Warfield, "Inspiration," 231.

[28] See Lindsell, *Battle for the Bible,* 31, 33; cf. Davis, *Debate About the Bible,* 29.

[29] Hodge and Warfield, "Inspiration," 250.

[30] See, for example, the definition given by Paul D. Feinberg, "The Meaning of Inerrancy" in Norman L. Geisler, *Inerrancy* (Grand Rapids: Zondervan, 1979), 294, quoted in R. D. Land, "A Conservative Response," 75.

raphy are made, they are without error,[31] because God preserved the authors of Scripture from error in those matters as well as in matters more properly pertaining to its central message of human salvation.

Error, as the word is used in this sense, does not refer to such trivial matters as a misspelled word or a mistake in grammar. Rather, an error is understood to be a misstatement or something contrary to fact. Because of the vulnerability of the assertion of errorlessness in the light of admitted discrepancies in parallel accounts of events in both Old and New Testaments, Hodge and Warfield formulated three tests that must be met before something can be called an error: it must occur without doubt in the "original autograph" of the book; the interpretation which allowed the error must be the true meaning and intention of that text "definitely and certainly ascertained"; and the true sense of the autograph must be "directly and necessarily incon-sistent" with some "certainly known" fact of history or truth of science.[32] Only when those three conditions were met would conservatives admit that Scripture contained an *error*.

One notices immediately that the discussion here concerns not the copies we possess of Scripture, not even our oldest manuscripts in the original languages, but the "autographs," that is, the documents that were originally written by the authors themselves. The doctrine of inspiration, therefore, for the conservatives, rightly applies only to those autographs.[33] Since no autograph is known to have survived, it would appear that the conservatives have not only an impregnable position—one cannot prove an error in something one does not possess—but also a highly dubious one. Of what use is an inerrant Scripture which is unavailable? In earlier times, it was possible to argue, as did the Westminster Confession (Sec. 1:8), that God had not only inspired Scripture but had maintained the purity of the text. The

---

[31] For example, Hodge and Warfield, "Inspiration," 237, 238, 251; Boice, ed., *Foundation of Biblical Authority*, 10, 19; Lindsell, *Battle for the Bible*, 182; *Chicago Statement*, par. 4 of "A Short Statement," cf. Davis, *Debate About the Bible*, 16, 31.

[32] For a definition of *error*, see Lindsell, *Battle for the Bible*, 36; the three rules appeared in Hodge and Warfield, "Inspiration," 242, and have, with variations, been widely repeated by conservative authors.

[33] *Chicago Statement*, art. X; cf. Rogers, ed., *Biblical Authority*, 39; Barr, *Fundamentalism*, 297, notes that this allows conservatives to deny any role to church tradition in the formation or preservation of Scripture.

discovery of a multitude of biblical manuscripts in the nineteenth and twentieth centuries, however, has made clear that no such wondrous preservation took place.[34] Nevertheless, conservatives affirm, the copies we have of the autographs are accurate enough as to be trustworthy. Modern textual criticism, in the view of some conservatives, has been so successful that we may call the product of their research the word of God.[35] Therefore, the conservative argues, we must accept everything recorded in Scripture—doctrine, science, history—and we must accept it as reliable and trustworthy, even if it may be denied by modern scientists.[36] A careful formulation of that position would affirm that Scripture, inerrant in its autographs, when properly interpreted is inerrant in all matters, including history and science. We will need to explore the implications of such a view below.

Obviously, however, if one holds the view that Scripture contains truth uncontaminated by any error, one would surely deem it important to show that Scripture itself has such a view of itself. At best, of course, the evidence is indirect, since the Bible is remarkably reticent about itself. As in all affirmations, the presupposition is at work that since God speaks through Scripture, and he cannot lie, Scripture cannot lie. References such as 2 Timothy 3:16, which says all Scripture is inspired by God; 2 Peter 1:20–21, which affirms that prophets moved by the Holy Spirit spoke from God; John 17:17, where Jesus says of God, "Thy word is truth" (equated with Scripture as "Word of God"); and John 10:34–35, where Jesus quotes Psalm 82:6 and then says that "scripture cannot be broken," are cited as evidence that inerrancy is the Bible's view of itself.[37] Another method of procedure is to argue that

---

[34] This of course does not prevent some conservatives from continuing the affirmation of the Westminster Confession, but enlightened conservatives have recognized the force of the manuscript discoveries.

[35] Text criticism is the act of comparing various texts of the same writing in an effort to determine which of the various readings can be explained as copying errors and which go back to the original author. Lindsell, *Battle for the Bible,* 37, displays great trust in the efforts of the text critics, as does Cottrell, "The Nature of Biblical Authority," 38, note 20. Boice, ed., *Foundation of Biblical Authority,* 88, argues that inerrancy of the autographs is the presupposition of text criticism; otherwise, why expend so much effort to recover the original? Such a view, needless to say, is not shared by all text critics.

[36] *Summit Papers,* 4.2.

[37] We shall have occasion to discuss these texts in more detail below.

since, according to the Gospels, Jesus regarded the Old Testament as "completely trustworthy, reliable and inerrant in matters of doctrine, history and science," we ought also to view both Old and New Testaments in the same light.[38] That is again based on the presupposition noted above, as applied to such statements as John 17:17 and 10:35; Jesus nowhere in any Gospel uses such words as *inerrant* or *science.*

Another justification frequently advanced for such a view of scriptural inerrancy is the affirmation that that view is the historic position of the church. The argument tends to rely more on repeated assertions of the truth of the affirmation than on quotations from various authors throughout the history of the church, but one can find statements in various periods of history that can be interpreted as supporting the view of inerrancy advocated by the conservatives.[39] It is certainly true that the idea of errorless Scripture was a prominent feature of Protestant as well as Catholic thought in the late seventeenth and early eighteenth centuries, the period of "Protestant Orthodoxy"; and it is in this period that the roots of the conservative view of Scripture lie.[40] It is also true, however, that the history of the church tends to support some form of the conservative view of Scripture more than it would tend to support, say, the liberal view, although, as we saw, liberals can also claim historic support for their view. In the last analysis, however, the presupposition of God as author of Scripture, a God incapable of lying, is far more important for the conservative argument for inerrancy than evidence found either in Scripture or in the history of the church.

The conservative emphasis on inerrancy as the key element in the inspiration of Scripture has ramifications in other areas that concern the way the Bible is understood and used, and we want now to

---

[38] Boice, ed., *Foundation of Biblical Authority*, 92; for a discussion of this point from a critical stance, see Barr, *Fundamentalism*, 260–61.

[39] See, e.g., Boice, ed., *Foundation of Biblical Authority*, 9, 16–17. Augustine's *Letter 82* to Jerome, par. 3, contains a favorite reference to canonical books as being free from error, and attributing what seems to be error to faulty manuscripts, translation errors, or inability to understand what is written (*Letters of Saint Augustine*, vol. 1 [ed. M. Dods, trans. J. G. Cunningham; Edinburgh: T&T Clark, 1972]).

[40] Reid, *Authority of Scripture*, 86, quotes Quenstedt, a Lutheran theologian of this period, in an affirmation of the errorlessness of Scripture. It could have been written by any modern conservative.

look at some of them. We will deal briefly with the authority and unity of the Bible, the certainty of faith based on it, and the way it is to be used and interpreted. This will shed light on how the conservative view of inspiration works itself out in these related areas.

Conservatives acknowledge of course that Christ is to be understood as the Word of God, but their strong emphasis on the Bible as the Word of God as well leads to an inclination either to affirm that there are two Words of God, or to affirm, practically if not theoretically, that the truly operative Word of God is the Bible. In that sense, the Bible and Christ coalesce into a single divine authority.[41] One can therefore say with no qualification that the Scriptures are in fact the Word of God, and as such they are of infallible divine authority in all matters they touch. So intimately related are Word of God and Bible, in fact, that it is possible to describe the study of Scripture by the phrase "probe God's mind."[42]

It is equally clear that for the conservative understanding, inerrancy is the sole basis for the authority of Scripture. To deny inerrancy for this way of understanding the Bible is to deny any authority of any kind to the Bible. Much of what raises the ire of conservative scholars is identified under the rubric of putting some other authority over Scripture by using it to judge whether or not Scripture may be understood as being inerrant. Whether such other authority be a bias against the supernatural or some kind of philosophical presupposition that would question inerrancy, conservatives are quick to point out that such an act not only questions inerrancy but denies the Bible its entire authority.[43]

---

[41] See Lindsell, *Battle for the Bible,* 30, who, in comparing Christ and the Bible as word of God, insists that "the Bible, then, is the Word of God." See also the *Chicago Statement,* Exposition, "Authority: Christ and the Bible." Perhaps for this reason, conservatives are fond of using the two-nature definition of Christ, divine and human, in relation to the Bible; for an example, see Lindsell, 34.

[42] The phrase is taken from Rogers, ed., *Biblical Authority,* 62; for an emphatic statement that Scriptures do not contain, but are the Word of God, see Hodge and Warfield, "Inspiration," 237.

[43] For example, Boice, ed., *Foundation of Biblical Authority,* 93; *Chicago Statement,* "A Short Statement," par. 5; for the position that denial of inerrancy is a denial of the Christian faith, see *Chicago Statement,* "Preface," par. 2. On the problem of another authority, see Lindsell, *Battle for the Bible,* the chapter entitled "Discrepancies in Scripture."

Similarly, with respect to revelation, conservatives are not satisfied with the idea that the Bible is a witness to revelation. It is not a witness to revelation, it is revelation, and therefore the Scriptures can be described as "revelation in writing." From that perspective, it is probably accurate to say that for the conservative point of view, inspiration and revelation are identical. It is the control exercised by divine inspiration which renders the Bible free from all error which also qualifies it as revelation.[44]

The manner in which conservatives understand inspiration provides them with a key point, in their view, for defending the certainty one may have in regard to faith's affirmations. Because inspiration understood as inerrancy guarantees an errorless Bible, inspiration provides the soundest basis for seeing the Bible as true and trustworthy in all matters. One of the major arguments that conservatives advance for their understanding of revelation centers around the idea that if one statement in the Bible is open to mistrust, one could no longer trust anything the Bible says. This idea is repeated again and again, both as affirmation and as a kind of threat: doubt one part of the Bible, and all parts are open to similar doubt. That pertains not only to matters of religion but to matters of history and science as well.[45] This understanding of the implication of inerrancy more than any other may perhaps explain the defensive, even bellicose nature of conservative arguments in regard to the inspiration of the Bible. At bottom, what is at stake is the right to be certain of the truth of the Christian faith. What is at issue is therefore not only the nature of inspiration, and hence of the Bible, but the right to have any confidence at all that Christian faith statements are true.

A corollary of this view concerns the relationship of inerrancy to the unity of the Bible. Since all parts of the Bible are equally inspired, all parts of the Bible are equally revelational. A major task of the conservative biblical student is therefore to demonstrate the total

---

[44] The phrase "revelation in writing" is from Rogers, ed., *Biblical Authority*, 61. *Chicago Statement*, art. III, denies the Bible is "merely a witness to revelation." For the judgment that inspiration and revelation are virtually identical, see Barth, *Conversation with the Bible*, 111.

[45] See Boice, ed., *Foundation of Biblical Authority*, 89, 203, as an example. For its practical application, see *Chicago Statement*, arts. IX and XIII; cf. also Rogers, ed., *Biblical Authority*, 38; Barr, *Fundamentalism*, 263.

inspiration and revelational quality of all Scripture by showing that what Scripture teaches is a unity. A great deal of effort is expended by conservative scholars in the task of demonstrating that apparent inconsistencies can in fact be harmonized with one another, thus displaying the unity of Scripture based on the inspiration and inerrancy of all of its parts.[46]

All of this, finally, has implications for the way in which Scripture is to be understood and interpreted. Obviously, if inspiration is understood to mean inerrancy, then to find error in Scripture is to have misunderstood or misinterpreted it. Conservatives are clear in their own mind that the "plain and obvious" meaning of the text, when found, will bear out the nature of Scripture as error free.[47] For that reason it is wrong to characterize conservatives as "literalists," as though they insist on an absolutely literal interpretation of the text. A glance at contemporary conservative exegesis shows this not to be the case. If a conservative insists that the ages attributed to the various figures in Genesis 5, including Methuselah, are to be taken literally, another will argue that the term *day* in the account of Creation (Gen. 1:1 to 2:4a) does not mean a twenty-four-hour period.[48] What is at issue is not the literal but the *intended* meaning of the text. In actual practice, the task of conservative interpretation is not to find the literal meaning, but rather to find that interpretation which allows one to continue to affirm the errorless nature of the passage, and of Scripture in general. If a literal understanding is preferred, a nonliteral understanding (as in the case of "day") will be quickly adopted when a literal interpretation brings the passage into conflict with some scientifically demonstrable fact. How could it be otherwise, if Scripture is understood to be errorless in all affirmations? Clearly, on this understanding, if a statement appears to contradict scientific fact, it must have been intended in some way other than literal.[49]

---

[46] See Hodge and Warfield, "Inspiration," 252; Lindsell, *Battle for the Bible,* 114; Boice, ed., *Foundation of Biblical Authority,* 79.

[47] Lindsell, *Battle for the Bible,* 37; cf. Hodge and Warfield, "Inspiration," 241.

[48] See Hodge and Warfield, "Inspiration," 246; Barr, *Fundamentalism,* 41–44, contains examples of the kind of exegesis from which I have drawn two (p. 44 for the ages, p. 41 for the "day").

[49] This point is also made in Barr, *Fundamentalism,* 41. On the need of conservatives to harmonize Scripture and scientific fact, see Davis, *Debate About the Bible,* 74.

Through all of this, what the conservative is seeking is what God wants to teach him or her through Scripture. Again and again, *doctrine* and *teaching* appear as key words in conservative discussions of the intention of Scripture. It is that interest in finding the correct *doctrines* in Scripture which leads to the impression, not entirely undeserved, that conservatives are interested primarily in propositional revelation, that is, that revelation is to be found in statements rather than in historic acts. If the Bible is the Word of God, and if, because of the way it is inspired, it is revelation rather than merely the witness to revelation, then it is quite logical that such revelation be found in statements, in teachings, which can then be formulated in terms of "God's propositional truth."[50] It is just those teachings around which conservatives seek, in faithfulness to God, to shape their lives.

STRENGTHS AND WEAKNESSES OF THE CONSERVATIVE VIEW

Whatever else one may want to say about the conservative approach to the Bible, it is clear that it is motivated by a desire to take the Bible with utmost seriousness as the only valid authority for faith and life. There is no hint here, as there was in the liberal view, that the Bible ought to come under the judgment of the totality of human experience. On the contrary, the conservatives see it as their task to place the whole of human experience under the judgment of the Word of God which they find so clearly expressed in the Bible. In that way, human experience is made subservient to the will of God, and the Christian confession of God's lordship is to take concrete form in the routine of everyday life. Finding no other authority for life beyond the Word of God totally and clearly expressed in the pages of Scripture, the conservative sees as the highest duty the realization of that Word within the tasks of common life. Any attempt to find in the biblical witness one element more important than all others, which enables one to understand God's intention for the world and for its people, is thus effectively countered. This unwillingness to acknowledge any lordship, moral or intellectual,

---

[50]The phrase is used in Boice, ed., *Foundation of Biblical Authority*, 11; Barr, *Fundamentalism*, 76, also emphasizes this didactic interest; his discussion made me sensitive to this element of conservative biblical understanding.

other than that of Scripture is perhaps the greatest strength of the
conservative view of the nature and inspiration of the Bible.

This view of the inspiration and hence of the authority of the
Bible has as its consequence a great seriousness about the actual text
of the Bible. Although in its early stages text criticism was not wel-
comed by those who held a more conservative view of the nature of
Scripture, that objection has long since been quieted, and in many
cases, it is precisely the conservatives who have continued the exacting
work of textual reconstruction. Indeed, the idea of an inerrant autograph provides the solid theological motivation for text-critical work
that is simply absent from more liberal views of the Bible. With such
an original, there is ample reason to want to find, to the best of human
critical ability, the very wording of that primal text.

None of this is to say that the conservative view we have sketched
out does not have a variety of problems inherent in the approach it
takes to the nature of Scripture, its inspiration and authority. Because
of the resurgence in recent times of the conservative outlook in regard
to Scripture, we will want to devote a good deal of space to a critique
of its views.

According to one of its proponents, the confession of scriptural
inerrancy commits us "in advance to harmonize and integrate all that
we find Scripture teaching, without remainder."[51] That means that the
presupposition about the nature of Scripture is fed into the interpretative process at the very outset, and any interpretation that might
threaten inerrancy must be ruled out in advance. That means, as we
shall see, that the hermeneutical principle of conservative exegesis is
scriptural inerrancy, and no method or conclusion may be tolerated
that would conflict with that principle.[52]

A second affirmation of those who hold the conservative approach consists in the claim that inerrantists take the Bible in its plain
and obvious sense.[53] That claim is accurate to the extent that it is meant

---

[51] Boice, ed., *Foundation of Biblical Authority*, 79.

[52] The remark of Robison B. James ("Authority, Criticism, and the Word of God,"
in R. B. James, ed., *The Unfettered Word: Southern Baptists Confront the Authority-Inerrancy
Question* [Waco, Tex.: Word Books, 1987], 83) is thus justified: "systematic inerrancy is
designed to be uncorrectable by anything it might find in the Bible." Abraham (*Divine
Inspiration*, 22) makes a similar point.

[53] E.g., Lindsell, *Battle for the Bible*, 37–38; cf. Barr, *Fundamentalism*, 53.

to counter the claim that conservatives are literalists and seek only the literal, as opposed to a symbolic or metaphorical understanding. As we alluded to earlier, the "obvious meaning" of the text is taken to be the literal meaning only when such a meaning does not threaten the principle of inerrancy.

A third point to note at the outset is the fact that inerrancy as applied to biblical interpretation means that to be inerrant, the biblical text must speak of reality in a way that conforms and corresponds to external reality as it appears to us in our commonsense view. Thus the Bible must not only be harmonized internally, to eliminate discrepancies and theological errors, it must also be harmonized externally so that it does not conflict with known and observable phenomena. If truth is one, and the Bible as God's Word is truth, then it cannot, by definition, conflict with assured results of modern science. No conservative, on the basis of biblical language, would seek to overthrow the heliocentric theory of astronomy and insist that the sun circles the earth. In a similar way, as we shall see, the meaning of the biblical text must be made to conform to the common assumptions we all make about the nature of reality. For that reason, what is "plain and obvious" to inerrantists often seems artificial and tortured to those whose primary goal in interpretation is something other than conformity to the principle of inerrancy.[54]

Given such presuppositions, it is obvious that one of the first tasks of conservative interpretation will be to show that Scripture contains no factual errors, i.e., statements that fail to conform to the external reality we know. On the admission of conservatives themselves, any single statement of such nature would invalidate the idea of the inerrant inspiration of Scripture.[55] Such an error must mean either that the Holy Spirit did not inspire it, in which case one must wonder where else uninspired statements occur, or that the Holy Spirit did inspire an error, in which case one must wonder how many other inspired statements are also erroneous. For

---

[54] This leads Abraham (*Divine Inspiration,* 29) to observe we must "either abandon the theology of inerrancy or we must abandon a natural and honest study of the Bible." For a good discussion of this whole point, see Barr, *Fundamentalism,* 49–53. Despite occasional overly negative language, the book as a whole is well worth reading.

[55] Hodge and Warfield, "Inspiration," 244.

that reason, any semblance of error is a great embarrassment to the conservative position.

That there are errors in the "plain and obvious" sense of Scripture has long been seen by those not committed to their denial. For example, Matthew 27:9–10 identifies a quotation as coming from Jeremiah which appears nowhere in that book, but has its closest parallel in Zechariah 11:12–13. All conservative attempts to link Jeremiah with Zechariah in Jerusalem, or to ascribe the quotation to an oral tradition (no such is known), or to piece together vaguely similar materials from a variety of places in Jeremiah, are clearly not motivated by an attempt to get at the plain sense of Matthew 27:9–10. They are attempts to preserve the text from what the conservatives perceive as an error.[56] Similarly, when Mark 1:2 identifies a quotation as coming from Isaiah, the "plain and obvious" sense would indicate that Mark thought Isaiah was its source. The presence in that quotation of words taken from Malachi 3:1, which precede the quotation from Isaiah, and the correction of the quotation in Matthew 3:3 (Matthew omits the material from Malachi), indicate that we have here an "error," recognized as such and corrected by a later Evangelist. That is a problem only to those for whom such an "error" would invalidate the primary presupposition about the nature of the Bible. A similar error occurs in Mark 2:26, where Abiathar is mistakenly identified as priest when David ate the bread of the Presence (it was Abiathar's son who was priest; see 1 Sam. 21:1–6; 2 Sam. 8:17). Another is found in Mark 4:31 when Jesus says the mustard seed is "the smallest of all the seeds on earth," a statement which is botanically in error.[57] Neither is earthshaking, but for one for whom inerrancy is an issue, and for whom Jesus must be omniscient (in itself a strange position in the light of

---

[56] For a discussion of this "problem," see Davis, *Debate About the Bible,* 102–4; Hodge and Warfield, "Inspiration," 259–60.

[57] On Mark 2:26, see Lindsell, *Battle for the Bible,* 166–67; on Mark 4:31, p. 169. On the latter passage, compare Davis, *Debate About the Bible,* 26, 107–8. Both passages have been "corrected" in the parallel material in Matthew and Luke: On Mark 2:26, see Matt. 12:4, Luke 6:4, where reference to Abiathar is omitted. On Mark 4:31, see Luke 13:19, where any reference to size is omitted, and Matt. 13:32, where the phrase "of all those on the earth" is omitted. Typically, conservatives like to deal with the Matthean version, since it is not so absolute a statement (see, e.g., Lindsell, *Battle for the Bible,* 169).

Mark 13:32), it presents a problem, and in its solution, the "plain" meaning of the text becomes tortured indeed.[58] The biologically false assertion in Leviticus 11:6 and Deuteronomy 14:7 that the hare chews a cud and is thus a ruminant, and the attempts to explain it away gave rise in the nineteenth century to a bit of sarcastic doggerel:

> The bishops all have sworn to shed their blood
> To prove 'tis true the hare doth chew the cud.
> O bishops, doctors, and divines, beware—
> Weak is the faith that hangs upon a hare.[59]

Examples of such "errors" could be multiplied, but the problem is posed by any of the examples given. In addition to the attempt to show that such statements are not in error, some conservatives have attempted to account for such material by arguing that although Jesus may have known, for example, that botanically the mustard seed was not the smallest, his listeners thought it was, so to make his point, Jesus "accommodated" the statement to his hearers' limited knowledge.[60] Although this would preserve Jesus from an unwitting error, and one could still perhaps argue that Jesus' intention in using this (erroneous) illustration was inerrant truth, it does not remove the "error." For that reason and others, this theory has not found particular favor with modern conservatives.[61]

One of the problems, of course, lies in the definition of *error*. It is one thing to find a statement that we now, with a different world view, recognize not to conform to our understanding of reality, and which therefore we would label an error. It is quite another thing to find a statement that intended to lead someone astray from what the author of the statement took to be the truth.[62] Where that distinction is not made, and it rarely is among conservatives, there is a confusion

---

[58] On the necessity of Jesus to be omniscient, see Lindsell, p. 45.

[59] Quoted from Davis, *Debate About the Bible*, 111.

[60] See Davis, *Debate About the Bible*, 41–46; cf. Berkouwer, *Holy Scripture*, 175. Similarly Calvin, who argued that God's Spirit accommodated himself to "mistaken, though generally received opinion" (quoted in Bloesch, *Holy Scripture*, 109).

[61] Boice, ed., *Foundation of Biblical Authority*, 93, where it is found objectionable.

[62] Jack Rogers ("The Church Doctrine of Biblical Authority" in Rogers, ed. *Biblical Authority* [Waco, Tex.: Word Books, 1977], 46) notes that confusing " 'error' in the sense of technical accuracy with the biblical notion of error as willful deception diverts us from the serious intent of Scripture."

between error as incorrectness and error in the sense of "sin and deception."[63] If Jesus erred intentionally, with the desire to conceal the truth in comparing the kingdom of God with the growth of a small seed such as that of the mustard plant, it is a serious matter. If, on the other hand, as a first-century Jew, Jesus incorrectly assumed the seed of the mustard plant to be the smallest and used it to illustrate what he knew to be a true statement, it is difficult to see a problem, unless, of course, one's goal in all interpretations is not to find the intention of the text, but to define that intention in such a way that it supports the prior assumption of total inerrancy. The fact that conservatives have tended in some cases to admit the possibility of errors in Scripture in the sense of "incorrect statements," which do not affect the intent to tell a larger truth, leads one to suspect that the attempt to defend Scripture as totally errorless is covertly recognized to be the unrewarding task it obviously is.[64]

A second major problem for advocates of an inerrant, and thus theologically harmonious and doctrinally homogeneous, Scripture is posed by any potential inconsistency between any two passages of Scripture. Absence of such agreement would also be a fatal blow to the conservative position that inspired Scripture must necessarily be inerrant.[65] Since on the "plain" meaning of the text, there are discrepancies, the conservative interpreter is obliged either to show a different meaning of the text which eliminates the discrepancy (thus "harmonizing" the texts), or to deny the existence of the discrepancy. To gain an idea of the dimensions of the problem, a few commonly noted discrepancies may be listed.

Both Jesus and Paul pointed to discrepancies in their Scriptures, i.e., the Old Testament. On the basis of the discussion in Galatians 3:1–12, it appears that Paul thought Habakkuk 2:4 and Leviticus 18:5 were mutually exclusive and represented the correct and incorrect ways of finding life. The discussion of marriage in Matthew 19:3–9 indicates that Jesus thought Deuteronomy 24:1 needed to be corrected by Genesis 1:27; 2:24, thus indicating a discrepancy between those two

---

[63] I am borrowing terms from Berkouwer, *Holy Scripture,* 181; cf. also Rogers, ed., *Biblical Authority,* 46, 168; Beegle, *Scripture, Tradition, and Infallibility,* 148–49.

[64] See the discussion of Hodge and Warfield in Rogers, ed., *Biblical Authority,* 110–11; cf. also pp. 64–65; Davis, *Debate About the Bible,* 26–27.

[65] See as an example Hodge and Warfield, "Inspiration," 236.

passages.[66] There are in addition a variety of discrepancies and inconsistencies in the Bible, within the Old Testament, between the Old and New Testaments, and within the New Testament. A few examples will make clear the kind of problem facing us. There are, for example, statistical discrepancies: in 2 Samuel 10:18, David killed 700 Aramean chariot warriors, in 1 Chronicles 19:18 he killed 7,000 in the same battle; in 2 Samuel 24:24, David bought a threshing floor for 50 shekels of silver, in 1 Chronicles 21:25 the price was 600 shekels of gold; in Numbers 25:9, 24,000 died in a plague, in 1 Corinthians 10:8, the number is set at 23,000; in Genesis 15:13, God predicts Abraham's descendants will be enslaved in Egypt 400 years, in Exodus 12:41, the report puts the time span at 430 years (Paul in Gal. 3:17 prefers the number given in Exodus). Such discrepancies are of course common in any literature, ancient or modern, where more than one account of the same event is recorded. For a view that says this literature was inspired and hence is error free, however, they represent a real problem. Some attempts have been made to explain them: round numbers were used and were rounded off differently by different authors; or biblical standards of exactness were alien to ours; or inerrancy does not imply modern standards of precision; or accuracy, not exactness, is the test of inerrancy.[67] All these statements are, of course, true, but they amount to a weakening of the meaning of inerrancy to the point that calling such material "error free" is emptied of its content. If disagreement on reports of identical events does not mean that at least one of the reports is in error, it is difficult to take seriously the firm assertions of inerrancy made by conservatives on behalf of Scripture.

There are of course kinds of discrepancies other than the simply statistical. In 2 Samuel 24:1–2, God is the one who provokes a census of Israel; in 1 Chronicles 21:1–2, it is Satan. The numbers reported for the census also differ. To say that God provoked Satan to do his bidding in the account in 1 Chronicles is to find more in Scripture than is there,

---

[66] See N. A. Dahl, *Studies in Paul* (Minneapolis: Augsburg, 1977), 161, 164, 170. As he points out (pp. 162, 166–67), such discrepancies in the Old Testament were noted by both Philo (Num. 23:19 and Deut. 8:5) and Hillel (Exod. 12:5 and Deut. 16:2). It would not be surprising therefore if both Paul and Jesus assumed that discrepancies existed.

[67] See, respectively, Lindsell, *Battle for the Bible*, 168; Berkouwer, *Holy Scripture*, 228; *Chicago Statement*, "Infallibility, Inerrancy, Interpretation"; Hodge and Warfield, "Inspiration," 239.

an act condemned by conservatives when others do it. According to Genesis 1:26, man is the last thing God created; in Genesis 2:7, man is the first. Historical discrepancies can be found between the accounts of when Abraham's father died (Acts 7:4 and Gen. 11:32; 12:4), and the account of where Jacob was buried and who sold Abraham the burial site (Acts 7:15–16 and Gen. 50:13; 23:16–18; cf. Josh. 24:32).

Old Testament quotations in the New also constitute a special problem. Often the quotation is quite free, thus raising the question, if the whole of Scripture is equally inspired, which text, the one in the Old Testament or the differing form in the New Testament, is the one to be believed? An even more difficult problem is raised when a New Testament author quotes not from the Hebrew Old Testament but from the Greek translation of it (called the Septuagint) and when the point of the New Testament author depends on something in the Greek translation which is not in the Hebrew original. For example, the point being made in Hebrews 10:5–9 depends on the Septuagint reading of Psalm 40:6–8, which says: "A body you have prepared for me" rather than the Hebrew original, which reads: "You have given me an open ear."[68] The same is true of the quotation of Psalm 16:10 in Acts 2:26–28. Whereas the Hebrew speaks of God keeping the faithful servant from the "pit," the Septuagint translation speaks of keeping the "Holy One" from "corruption," a change that lies at the heart of the point Peter is making in this sermon. The prophecy of Jesus' resurrection depends on the Septuagint translation, which is again different than the Hebrew original.[69] When Paul quotes "Scripture" in Romans 4:3, what he quotes is closer to the Septuagint than to the original Hebrew version of Genesis 15:6.

What is one to conclude from this? That the Septuagint is also inspired? Then we have two inspired versions of the Old Testament that differ from one another—at times significantly. Or are only those parts of the Septuagint inspired that are quoted in the New Testament? But then what of the Old Testament quotations in the New that do not reflect the Septuagint but which, though closer to the Hebrew, still differ? Which is the inspired version? To say that New Testament

---

[68] See the discussion of this point in Beegle, *Scripture, Tradition, and Infallibility,* 169. The same is true of the quotation of Ps. 8:5 in Heb. 2:7, see Berkouwer, *Holy Scripture,* 224–25.

[69] See Berkouwer, *Holy Scripture,* 223–24.

authors quote freely from the Old is tantamount to admitting that the New Testament authors did not treat the Old Testament as inerrant Scripture, something no conservative will willingly admit. What conservative would feel free to quote a biblical text so loosely and yet claim to be quoting Scripture?

A further problem lies in the discrepancies among the various Gospel reports of what Jesus said and did. In Mark 6:8–9, in giving instructions to his disciples relating to their journey as missionaries, Jesus tells them, among other things, to take a staff and wear sandals; in Matthew 10:9–10 he says take no staff and no sandals. The example could be multiplied many times over. There are discrepancies in events. In Mark (followed by Matthew and Luke), the cleansing of the temple by Jesus occurs during his final days in Jerusalem prior to his crucifixion. In John, it occurs among the first events of his public ministry, perhaps three years prior to his death. Trying to solve such problems by positing two temple cleansings or two instructions to the disciples gets one into such problems as having to posit six miraculous feedings, since there are six accounts of that event in the Gospels, and all differ from one another in detail (two each in Mark and Matthew; one each in Luke and John). On that basis, the inability of the disciples to cope with a hungry multitude borders on the miraculous itself—after five such feedings could they still have wondered how to deal with them (cf. Mark 6:35–36; 8:4; Matt. 14:17; 15:33; Luke 9:13; John 6:7)? And what is one to do then with the discrepancies in the account of the crucifixion? The multiple-event solution simply will not work. Either one agrees that, as in the case of the crucifixion, details can differ in the telling of one event, in which case it is difficult to posit more than one temple cleansing, or one must be consistent and say that every differing description indicates a different event. The former denies inerrancy by admitting the possibility of error in some account or the other; the latter is reduced to absurdity when confronted by the differing accounts of Jesus' death and resurrection.

Perhaps of more significance are the theological discrepancies. Can a God who caused inspired authors to write the saying of Jesus in Matthew 5:44 and Luke 6:27–28, with its gracious attitude even toward enemies, also have inspired the vindictive and almost malicious words of Psalm 109? Can the God who forbids the murder of one individual (Exod. 20:13; Luke 18:20; Rom. 13:9; cf. Gen. 9:6) really also have ordered the total slaughter of whole Canaanite settlements, including men, women, children, and cattle (Josh. 10:28–32)? Can the God whose sympathy is particularly upon widows, aliens, and fatherless children (Exod. 22:21–22) not only have permitted slavery (21:1–11) but even denied female slaves the seventh-year release granted to male slaves (v. 7)?[70]

Obviously, if the claim of inerrant, and thus harmonious, Scripture is to be upheld, this kind of discrepancy must be resolved. Aside from occasional attempts simply to ignore the inconsistent details and continue to affirm inerrancy; or to try to speak of faithful (and thus inerrant) recording of faulty sources (but how does that remove the errors that were present in those sources, however faithfully they were copied by the authors of Scripture?); or to differentiate between an infallible account, say, of what Jesus said, and an infallible account of what the author intended to say (but if the author's intention differed from the reality of what Jesus actually said, what is the significance of inerrancy at all?);[71] the major attempt to resolve discrepancies lies in what is called "harmonizing." This phenomenon deserves careful scrutiny.

The presuppositions that inform conservative interpretation of Scripture—the need to demonstrate inerrancy and the understanding that inerrancy means conformity to objective reality—are the presuppositions that also underlie the harmonizing of divergent passages. If it is possible to show that seemingly discrepant accounts can be reconciled by showing that they are only partial accounts of an actual event, the conservative interpreter is satisfied that he or she has shown the Bible to be "true" because it conforms inerrantly to external reality. Most attempts at harmonizing, and they are as numerous as the discrepancies within Scripture, are attempts therefore to show how discrepancies could be accounted for if the event to which they point could be constructed in a certain way.

The example of the denial of Jesus by Peter illustrates how this system works and the problems involved in it. The issue concerns how many times the cock will crow before Peter has denied Jesus three times. In Mark 14:30, Jesus tells Peter that before the cock crows twice,

---

[70] See the excellent discussion in *Canon and Authority,* ed. by G. W. Coats and B. O. Long (Philadelphia: Fortress, 1977), 126, from which I drew the example.

[71] For a cataloging of these and other attempts to resolve the problem, see Barr, *Fundamentalism,* especially chs. 3 and 10.

Peter will have denied him three times. Matthew 26:34, Luke 22:34, and John 13:38 portray Jesus as telling Peter that before the cock crows, the threefold denial will have occurred. In the event itself, Mark records the second crowing as the time of Peter's realization of what he has done (i.e., denied Jesus three times) in Mark 14:72, while, true to their accounts, Matthew (26:74), Luke (22:60), and John (18:27) simply record that the cock crowed, clearly implying that that was the first time this happened. Such divergence raises for the conservative the problem of how to reconcile accounts in which there is no agreement on how many times the cock crowed prior to Peter's denial. Conservatives solve the problem by constructing an event, using all four accounts, in which each of the accounts represents a partial view. In this case, Lindsell proposes that what actually happened was not a threefold, but a sixfold denial, with three denials preceding the first crowing (as in Matthew, Luke, and John), a further three preceding the second (as in Mark). In that way, Lindsell claims, he has proved "the honesty and accuracy of all four evangelists."[72] Yet what he has in fact demonstrated is just the opposite. If what he has constructed is the actual course of events, then *none* of the Gospels has given a true picture of objective reality. He has thus convincingly demonstrated that none of the four is inerrant, since none of them know what *really* happened, i.e., six denials. All claim three. To the argument that we need all four accounts to determine what really happened, and thus to justify their individual inerrancy, we must ask, what of those events where only one account is present? If no one Evangelist was completely correct in the account of this event, how do we know we have the correct event when there is only one Gospel account? One can of course argue that God has taken care to see that where there was only one Gospel account, it gave the total story, whereas such accuracy was not necessary when there was more than one, but that is tantamount to arguing

---

[72] Lindsell, *Battle for the Bible,* 174–76. To argue that Mark is "more specific" than Matthew or Luke, and to claim that one thus resolves the discrepancy, is really to claim that Matthew and Luke are not so careful as Mark, with the implication that in this instance, at least, Mark is more inerrant than the other two; see *Summit Papers,* 4.16, cf. also 4.8. But to argue that six denials really happened, while the Gospels are unanimous in recording three, is in fact to say that all four Gospels are in error, since not one records what "really happened." See Davis, *Debate About the Bible,* 35–37, for more on this point.

that the actual text of the Gospel, in its "plain meaning," is inerrant only when it presents information not contained in the other Gospel accounts. Of course such a view of "inerrancy" will be totally unsatisfactory to the conservative, but that is in fact the clear implication of the strategy of "harmonizing."

It is instructive to compare this method of salvaging inerrancy with the criticisms leveled by the same conservatives against modern critical methods of investigating Scripture. The criticism is that whereas conservatives "have always agreed that the writers of Scripture penned straight history," those who follow the historical-critical methods claim that the "biblical accounts are not true history," but that "one must go beyond the accounts in Scripture to find out what lies behind them."[73] Yet that is exactly what that very same author has done to "prove" that the Gospel accounts of Peter's denials are "true." He has located the story that no one Gospel tells, but that lies behind all four, thus proving they are "true history" by denying that any one account is a true account of all that happened. Such an implication lies behind every attempt to harmonize Scripture by pointing to a larger event underlying the various accounts, of which the passage of Scripture gives but a portion. In every case, the harmonizer is seeking to justify the truth of Scripture by going behind Scripture itself to an event that "lies behind it."

Another problem to be solved by harmonizing occurs when two passages in Scripture seem to contradict each other, and a solution cannot be found by such reconstruction. An example is the case of Jesus' ascension, which according to Luke 24:51 clearly appears to have occurred on Easter, while in Acts 1:3 it is reported as having occurred forty days after Easter. Since both verses plainly refer to the total event of the ascension, and it is difficult to say it took place over a forty-day period, literal truth is assigned to one passage (in this case, Acts), while the other, it is averred, "telescoped" the account and hence is less precise.[74] Here, by sacrificing the literality of one account (Luke), "inerrancy" is preserved for the other. One has here made a choice, since harmonization is not possible, and regarded one event as "his-

---

[73] Lindsell, *Battle for the Bible,* 205.

[74] I. H. Marshall, *The New Bible Commentary Revised,* 925; cited in Barr, *Fundamentalism,* 57.

tory" and the other, as it were, "interpretation." Thus, the "plain meaning" of Luke is sacrificed in the interest of preserving the inerrancy of the Acts account. Such ingenuity is frequently required if one is to elicit the "plain meaning" from discrepant witnesses who cannot be harmonized by hypothetical historical reconstruction.

In addition to the self-contradiction inherent in this policy of harmonizing, namely, that to "save" the truth of Scripture, an event is constructed which renders every account untrue as it stands, there is a second self-contradiction involved. That second self-contradiction concerns the problem of putting reason in a position where it becomes a court of appeal beyond the text of Scripture. It is of course precisely on this point that conservatives have attacked the liberal, critical view of Scripture. Conservatives see this principle at work both in the denial of inerrancy and in the denial of the miraculous. In both instances, they charge, critical reason has set itself above Scripture and is able to decide what in Scripture is true and what is not,[75] a procedure no conservative would permit to happen.

Yet conservative exegesis again and again manifests precisely this application of critical reason to the understanding of Scripture. For example, the Bible speaks frequently of God's "repenting" of some act or purpose (e.g., Gen. 6:6; Exod. 32:14; Judg. 2:18; 1 Sam. 15:35; 2 Sam. 24:16; Jer. 26:13; Amos 7:6; Jonah 3:10). Yet a God who is reliable must be unchangeable, which the Bible also asserts. When this problem is resolved by affirming that to say God "repents" is accommodation, whereas to say he is unchangeable is "how it is," one has not drawn this difference from the biblical text. When another conservative author says we are forbidden to "deny, disregard, or arbitrarily relativize" anything found in Scripture, he could easily have had the first commentator in mind. How did that first commentator decide that speaking of God's "repenting" is the accommodation (i.e., how it appears to us)? How does he know that the language of God's unchangeableness is not accommodation, with God's repenting "how it really is"? Clearly, some other source than Scripture itself has led him to this conclusion. Some other "authority" has allowed him to decide which Scripture is accommodation and which

---

[75] See, e.g., Lindsell, *Battle for the Bible*, 39–40, 163; *Chicago Statement*, the section titled "Inerrancy and Authority."

is literal description of actual reality.[76] Clearly, he has used his critical faculties in making such a decision.

The same displacement of the biblical witness by critical reason is at work every time a conservative author tries to "prove" that a narrative of some miraculous activity is "true" by arguing that it could have come about by natural causes of which we have analogies. For example, to argue that the flood cannot have covered all the earth, since to cover Mt. Everest would require water six miles deep over all the earth, which in turn presents an insurmountable problem of where the water went when the flood ended, and thus to argue that what we have is really a local flood of the Mesopotamian valley, is clearly to set reason above the scriptural account. Yet that is precisely the explanation offered by at least one conservative commentator.[77] To argue that the wondrous crossing of the Jordan River reported in Joshua 3:13–17 was made possible by a landslide which blocked the flow of water, as also occurred in A.D. 1266 and 1927, is clearly to deny the miraculous nature of the story and to put reason above the clear intention of the biblical narrative.[78] To argue that of the ten plagues in Egypt (Exod. 7:14 to 12:36) only the last was not due to perfectly natural phenomena that would accompany an inundation of the Nile valley (flagellates redden the river, cause fish to die which drive frogs ashore which are infected with Bacillus anthracis, which infected cattle; pools of water bred mosquitoes, rotting fish bred flies, etc.) in order to make credible those events and so "save" the inerrant truth of the accounts is as much to deny the miraculous through an appeal to "reason" as any attempt ever made by a "liberal" scholar.[79] Such examples are by no means isolated cases. They arise from the attempt to show how events recorded in the Bible could be "true" on the basis of a reconstruction of the event in the light of modern scientific knowledge. In the process, the intention of the text, which is to report a "miracle," is simply overturned. God's direct intervention becomes at best indirect, and his saving, wondrous acts are reduced to a matter of timing. Natural events occur at appropriate times, thus allowing

---

[76] The first comment is drawn from Boice, ed., *Foundation of Biblical Authority,* 25; the second from p. 77.

[77] Bernard Ramm, cited in Barr, *Fundamentalism,* 94–96.

[78] Hugh J. Blair, cited in Barr, *Fundamentalism,* 239–40.

[79] K. A. Kitchen, cited in Barr, *Fundamentalism,* 241–42.

God's plan to be set forward. That such a device was adopted by the "rationalists" of the eighteenth and nineteenth centuries to show how absurd it was for the Bible to claim that such events were "miracles" seems not to disturb these conservative interpreters.[80]

An appeal to an errorless autograph of Scripture to account for errors and discrepancies in our copies of the Bible is a further example of allowing reason to stand in judgment over Scripture. That the original copies of the various books in our canon, as they came from the pens of their respective authors, were free of all errors and discrepancies is a pure postulate. The Bible nowhere claims that to be the case, and no autograph exists to allow the postulate to be tested. The text of Scripture as we now possess it, even in the best critical editions, contains errors and discrepancies of the type we outlined above. Yet the conservative scholars, again and again, will appeal to this hypothetical original to justify the further postulate that God inspired an error-free Scripture. This is clearly to place a construct of reason, in this case theological reason, over the actual text of Scripture.[81] It has been frequently pointed out that if God thought errorless Scripture important enough to inspire its composition, he would surely also have further inspired its copying, so that it might remain error free.[82] Surely a God who can inspire error-free composition could also inspire error-free copying.[83] Since he did not, it would appear he did not think our possession of error-free Scripture very important.[84] But if it is not

---

[80] A convenient account of the rationalist views can be found in Albert Schweitzer, *The Quest of the Historical Jesus,* chs. 3 through 6 (New York: Macmillan, 1910), 27–67.

[81] Since conservatives will identify copying errors in places where there is no textual evidence that a variant reading ever existed at that point, the postulate of such errors is more a construct of reason than an evaluation of available evidence.

[82] Turretin did in fact affirm such preservation: "Nor can we readily believe that God, who dictated and inspired each and every word of these inspired men, would not take care of their entire preservation" (quoted in Rogers, "The Church Doctrine of Biblical Authority," 30).

[83] E.g., Clark Pinnock, "Three Views of the Bible in Contemporary Theology," in Rogers, ed., *Biblical Authority* (Waco, Tex.: Word Books, 1977), 66; Gnuse, *Authority of the Bible,* 32.

[84] Pinnock ("Three Views of the Bible," 65) points out that if only a flawless Bible is trustworthy, and we have no flawless Bible, since we have no autograph, the logical conclusion would be we must cease to trust the Bible we have.

important for us, why was it important originally? To suggest that God allowed the autographs to perish lest they be a temptation to idolatry is simply foolish.[85] Error-free copies would serve the same purpose as error-free originals, and those who would succumb to idolatry of an error-free original will, in its absence, find other things to idolize.

In saying that all such discrepancies and errors are due to copying, which has perverted the pristine original, conservatives lay themselves open to another problem: if God inspired error-free autographs, while the copies we have are no longer error free, how can we trust the copies we have? Will not error-laden copies engender the same distrust, so far as our access to God's true will is concerned, as originals that were not error free? The answer of the conservative is to assure the questioner that the authority of Scripture is not jeopardized by textual errors because God has in fact preserved our copies from major errors.[86] God's providence, in other words, incapable of producing copies free of all errors, has at least produced copies free of all major errors. That of course simply reintroduces the original problem: if the Bible we have is well enough preserved to be trustworthy, even with its errors and discrepancies that were not in the original, why all the fuss over inerrant autographs? Conservatives themselves will agree that saving faith does not have to include the proposition that Scripture is, or was, inerrant, nor does our faith depend on access to the inerrant autographs. But if God has used errant copies of Scripture to bring knowledge of his saving truth to generations of Christians, as he continues to use errant preachers to proclaim his word (and even errant scholars to announce the truth concerning inerrant autographs), why the postulate of inerrant originals? God doesn't need them to save us. We don't need them to appropriate that salvation. Why then do the conservatives need the postulate? Even the Scriptures used by Jesus and Paul, which by conservative estimate they regarded as inerrant, were surely copies. If copies containing errors were sufficient for Jesus and Paul, with no reference ever to some inerrant autograph, why are they not sufficient for us, without any such reference? If God can communicate through errant spelling and grammar, which conserva-

---

[85] A suggestion put forward by Lindsell, *Battle for the Bible,* 36.

[86] Barr, *Fundamentalism,* 36; Boice, ed., *Foundation of Biblical Authority,* 87; *Chicago Statement,* "Transmission and Translation"; *Summit Papers,* 7.34.

tives admit could be present even in texts they could regard as inerrant, why could God not originally have communicated through
Scriptures errant, from our perspective, in factual matters such as the
number of troops in a battle, or the years between entry into and exit
from Egypt, or the ancestors of Jesus? If God saves us through errant
copies, why insist that inspiration can be true only if the inspired works
were inerrant? Are conservatives not in fact insisting on more than
God evidently thinks necessary? Is not such an attitude indeed tantamount to putting a postulate of reason (inerrancy of autographs)
above the actual witness of Scripture?[87]

One is faced, in the end, with the question about the theological
usefulness, as well as the validity, of the conservative doctrine of the
inerrancy of Scripture in its original autographs. It is clear enough that
such inerrancy is not a central, or even peripheral, concern of Scripture itself. No definition of the inerrancy of autographs is offered in
the Bible, nor does any author deal with it in terms of his own work,
or even hint at it.[88] It is easier to find hints of fallibility on the part of
biblical authors (e.g., 1 Cor. 1:14–16) than any indication that what
they wrote is without the slightest error in the kind of detail that
worries adherents of the theory of inerrancy. The idea of the inerrancy
of scriptural autographs is therefore brought to Scripture, it is not
derived from it, in itself a telling comment on the way this conservative doctrine has developed.

It is very likely that because that is the case, conservatives dis-
claim any idea of the salvific necessity of the ideal of biblical inerrancy.[89] Nor does the truth of Christianity depend on such a notion
about Scripture. Conservatives concede that the truth of Christianity
would remain "even if God had not been pleased to give us, in addition
to His revelation of saving truth, an infallible record of that revelation
absolutely errorless, by means of inspiration."[90] Indeed there is no

---

[87] Although the formulation of these questions is my own, I have drawn on
material from Beegle, *Scripture, Tradition, and Infallibility*, 157–59, 164–65; Davis, *Debate
About the Bible*, 64, 79–80; Barr, *Fundamentalism*, 315; Rogers, ed., *Biblical Authority*, 66.

[88] For a good discussion of this point, see Davis, *Debate About the Bible*, 51–61.

[89] See most recently the *Chicago Statement*, art. XIX.

[90] The quotation is from Hodge and Warfield, "Inspiration," 227. That the idea of
inerrancy is based on assertion rather than evidence is clearly reflected in this
language.

logically compelling reason why "inspiration" can be held only if the product is an "absolutely errorless" Scripture. God has used, and continues to use, fallible human beings for the purposes of announcing his will, and we are hardly in a position to say how God had to produce Scripture. Inerrancy as a postulate derives not so much from the idea that the Bible is inerrant—indeed the evidence against it is all but overwhelming, driving its adherents to posit an unavailable proof, the autographs—as apparently from the idea that it must be inerrant.[91] One can only ask why that must be so, if Scripture does not itself teach it, salvation does not depend on it, and the truth of Christianity can stand without it.

Over against this debate about the necessity, or even the usefulness, of the idea of scriptural inerrancy must be placed the disadvantage it brings with it, namely, the dislocation of the true center of concern. The debate about and defense of inerrancy, with its endless attempts to reconcile what at best are peripheral details, diverts attention from the central themes of Scripture. Like the scribes who tithe mint and dill but neglect the weightier matters of the law (Matt. 23:23), defenders of inerrancy spend far too much time trying to reconstruct events supposedly underlying Scripture which in their minds then allows them to claim that inerrancy is "proved." It is, finally, foolish to make the authority of Scripture depend on the rabbit's cud or the disciples' sandals. Diversion of attention from the Bible's witness about God's saving acts to questions about the precise accuracy of minor details is, in the end, perhaps the most serious defect in the conservative equation of inspiration of Scripture with its supposed inerrancy.[92]

A final observation must be made about the understanding of inspiration we have been discussing. Underlying all the conservative discussion of the nature of inspiration and its eventuation in an error-free Scripture, there is the tacit assumption that such inspiration is

---

[91] See the discussion of this and similar points in Rogers, ed., *Biblical Authority,* esp. 64–65.

[92] There are other problems with the claims of the defenders of inerrancy: it is in fact not the historic position of the church; its reduction of Scripture to one level of value with its claim that all parts are equally inspired and so equally valid as doctrine, cannot be discussed here for lack of space. Problems which are for the conservative view inherent in the development of the canon will be discussed below.

best understood by means of the prophetic model. That is, inspiration is to be understood as occurring in the mind and heart of individuals who, moved by God's Spirit, write down what God desires to have recorded in that particular portion of Holy Scripture. However the actual process of inspiration be understood—whether it be thought of in terms of the dictation of every word[93] or only in the excluding of all error, whether the inspiration is to be located in the person or in the words that person writes, whether accommodation to the limits of the readers has occurred, either as conscious device or as divine purpose unknown to that particular author—in understanding the biblical autographs to be inerrant, the conservative pictures Scripture as written on the prophetic model of inspiration.

The same is true in large measure of the liberal position we reviewed. Whatever disagreement the liberals may have with conservatives on the matter of inerrancy and the consequent nature of Scripture and the way it is to be used, there is tacit if not conscious agreement that Scripture as it now stands is the work of individual authors, who produced the various literary works that now comprise our Bible.

It is just that model of inspiration, however, shared in large measure by conservative and liberal alike,[94] which has been called into question by scholarly discoveries made over the past few decades about the way Scripture was produced. Our next task, therefore, is to survey the way modern critical scholars view Scripture, to see what light that sheds on the way we ought to understand the nature of Scripture and hence the mode of its inspiration. Drawing on those insights, we will then be in a position to attempt the formulation of a way of understanding the inspiration of Scripture that takes into account what we now perceive to be the way in which our Scriptures were in fact produced.

---

[93] For an excellent discussion of such direct dictation as the covert but essential presupposition to any theory of inerrancy, see Abraham, *Divine Inspiration,* esp. 34–35.

[94] An indication of the pervasiveness of this model for understanding inspiration may be seen in the carefully reasoned book by Karl Rahner, *Inspiration in the Bible* (trans. C. H. Henkey; Freiburg: Herder & Herder, 1961), where, although the prophetic model is never formally discussed, it is presumed throughout.

Chapter 3

How the Scriptures
Were Formed

Perhaps the most important single issue that separates the modern critical view of Scripture from that of the conservatives lies in the fact that critical scholars take Scripture far more literally. That is, critical scholars are not so much perturbed by discrepancies and errors which a preconceived notion of the nature of Scripture would force them to explain away or harmonize, as they are interested in accounting for them. The difference between the critical view of Scripture and the conservative view is therefore not that the conservatives take the text "literally" while others do not. As we saw above, when discrepancies would result from the literal, face-value reading of the text, the conservative has recourse immediately to a harmonizing process in which one or both of the texts have their literal meaning subordinated to an explanation of the text that will preserve inerrancy: the copyist has made an error, ancient standards of accuracy were different from ours, some event can be constructed which allows both accounts to be true as parts of the total event. These and other explanations are adopted to account for the phenomena of Scripture which, on their face, would render difficult if not untenable the idea of inerrancy.

BIBLE BOOKS FROM EARLIER SOURCES

Instead of constructing such explanations of Scripture to save some prior notion of what Scripture is like, critical scholars, noting that secular literature from the ancient world frequently developed from oral accounts or from the combination of a number of sources, ask whether that may not also be the case with the literature contained in our Bible. When discrepancies exist, could it be that the discrepant details come from differing accounts, or different sources, which have been combined in our biblical books? When accounts in the Synoptic Gospels differ, could it be that further theological reflection by the community has found a way to phrase an account which allows the point to be made in such a way that irrelevant questions are avoided? When, for example, Mark says that Jesus went to share in John's baptism of repentance for the remission of sin (Mark 1:4–5, 9), would one not assume Jesus too shared such repentance for sins he had committed? Yet that surely is not what the story intends to say. When Matthew then records John's objections to his baptizing Jesus (Matt. 3:13–15), the reformulation may be aimed precisely at eliminating speculation about what sins Jesus might have committed that led him to be baptized. Again, when Genesis 17:25 says Ishmael was thirteen years old when Isaac was born, but Genesis 21:14–15 assumes Ishmael was a babe in arms when Hagar was driven into the wilderness after the birth of Isaac, we have rather clear evidence that the account of Abraham and Hagar has been constructed of various stories that originated independently of one another. In such ways, taking the text "literally" leads to the suggestion that discrepancies in the various accounts are due to combinations of sources, and to their further theological development.

Before we investigate further evidence to support the critical hypothesis that such phenomena as we find in Scripture are best accounted for on the supposition that our biblical books are composed of varieties of traditions that have received differing formulations and interpretations, two points need to be made clear. First, the point of the biblical material is not primarily historical. It is primarily theological. Such historical accounts as there are, are told for the theological points they help to make. This is as true of the patriarchal accounts in Genesis as it is of the Gospels and Acts. Biblical materials are closer in intent to sermons than they are to textbooks of history. That is not to say that historical accounts are not present and that they are not on occasion remarkably accurate. It is simply to say that the traditions were formulated and the biblical books composed, not to pass on historical information, but to say something about the ways of God with humankind: in the Old Testament through the fate of the chosen people, in the New Testament with the nascent church. To try to make the Bible speak as a historical chronicle is therefore to pervert its intention and to distort what it wants to convey.

The second point that needs to be made clear is simply that both critical and conservative scholars formulate constructs in the course of their exegesis. It is not the case that the conservatives take the Bible at its plain and literal meaning, while critical scholars impose theories of source development on Scripture. We saw clearly enough the willingness, even eagerness, of conservative scholars to construct hypothetical events that would then allow them to resolve to their satisfaction discrepancies that occurred in the text. One need think only of the proposal made to resolve the discrepancies of the four Gospel accounts about Peter's denial of Jesus (six times, rather than the unanimous Gospel witness of three times) to realize that conservatives are quick to construct explanations for Scripture that differ from the present text of Scripture. The difference between critical scholars and conservative scholars therefore does not lie in the willingness of one and the unwillingness of the other to impose alien constructs on Scripture. The difference lies in the kind of constructs that are created to account for the present shape of Scripture. Conservative constructs are dictated by the prior assumption that Scripture is inerrant, and whatever is necessary to produce to protect that assumption is produced. Critical scholars assume that when the same phenomena appear in the Bible and in other ancient literature, they have the same cause, and thus the scholars seek to isolate the various traditions that have been woven together in our Bible. Therefore, since both conservative and critical scholars are willing to construct hypotheses to account for the phenomena found in Scripture, the difference between them lies in the assumptions each brings to that Scripture. It is the burden of this chapter to show that the critical assumptions are truer both to the nature and to the intention of Scripture.

The assumption, then, that critical scholars feel has been forced upon them by the nature of the biblical literature is that that literature has been composed in many instances of the combination of earlier traditions; that in the transmission of those traditions as well as in their combination, theological reflection and appropriation have continued to occur; and that Scripture therefore reflects the dynamic process at work in the community of Israel, and in the church, as those who stood within these communities sought to understand the significance of their God-directed history. The evidence leading to such an assumption the critical scholar finds overwhelming. We can review only a small fraction of it.

The fact that the biblical books are based on prior sources is in some instances stated by the biblical book itself. Thus, for example, we learn that some of the material in 1 and 2 Kings was drawn from the "Book of the Chronicles of the Kings of Israel" (1 Kgs. 15:31; 16:20; 2 Kgs. 10:34; 13:8), and that what was taken was only a selection from that literature. Closer analysis of those books has shown that the historical material is used in the service of a larger, theological purpose, namely, to show that the fate of kings and nations is determined more by their faithfulness to God than by the extent of their national wealth or the size of their armies. The selection from the sources therefore had theological rather than historical intent. Again, the Gospel of Luke begins with an account of the source material available (Luke 1:1—from the material in Luke it seems apparent that one of those "many" narratives was the Gospel of Mark), and hints that for this author, that material was in some sense deficient (1:3–4). Recent research on Luke has made abundantly clear that the purpose of that Gospel also is theological rather than simply historical. Selection of material from available sources is also hinted at in Mark 4:33 (reference to other parables not included) and 6:56 (reference to healings not described), and is made explicit in John 20:30 and 21:25. The selection in John is made expressly for a theological purpose (20:31—to awaken faith).

In other instances, careful analysis of the biblical book itself indicates that it has been assembled from traditions which have been worked and reworked over a period of time by a variety of authors. The book of Judges is a clear example of such a process. From a variety of older stories about various heroes of the several tribes of Israel, an account has been constructed to show that neglect of the true God has fearsome consequences for his chosen people. That theme is set out in Judges 2:16–23. The careful reader will note the recurring pattern of disobedience, disaster, repentance, and rescue. From time to time there are hints that a king would solve such problems, since regal absence produces such chaos. That is the gist, for example, of the

closing sentence of the book. From such evidence, scholars have concluded that individual tribal stories were collected and arranged to
make a theological point (obedience to God is the critical issue) as well
as a political point (kings ensure stability). That political point itself,
however, has theological implications, namely, that kings (David is
the prime example) who obey God rescue their people.[1]

One can observe the same process at work in the book of Exodus.
There is, for example, a remarkable tension contained in a series of
regulations found in Exodus 21 to 23. One finds, on the one hand,
regulations that regard slaves as property of their master (21:1–11, 21),
that deny to female slaves the right to be released after six years of
service (21:7), that imply women are the property of their fathers, or,
if married, of their husbands (22:16–17; 21:8, 22), and that regard the
value of a human being as related to his or her status as slave or free
(21:23–25, 26–27, 29–31, 32). On the other hand, one finds regulations
that show compassion to aliens (22:21; 23:9), that are especially concerned with widows and fatherless children (22:22–24), that insist the
poor are not to be exploited (22:25–27) or suffer injustice (23:6), that
are even concerned lest animals be maltreated (23:11–12). Such a
contrast is probably best explained by assuming the combination of
two sources of regulations, the first tied to the status quo of the society
and reflecting normal cultural values of that time and place, while the
second, grounded in the special history of Israel (e.g., 23:9), transcends
such regulations and locates the basis of society in the same mercy and
justice of God that Israel has experienced in its own national life as
chosen people. The clash of divine mercy with conventional social
values points not to a static Scripture of eternal immutable laws, but
rather to a process whereby God's revelation of himself and his will is
taking command of Hebraic national life, the same process we can
observe in the prophets.[2]

In some cases, some books are simply rewritten forms of other
biblical books, done in an effort to make a new point. The books of

---

[1] This example of Judges, like all the others, has been greatly simplified because
of the limitations of space. The evidence itself can be found in any good
commentary, such as *Judges,* by Robert Boling, vol. 6A in the Anchor Bible, see pp.
29–38.

[2] I have excerpted and summarized here the excellent work contained in Coats
and Long, eds., *Canon and Authority,* esp. 115–25.

Chronicles, for example, are largely a recasting of 1 and 2 Kings, done in an effort to accent the importance of the temple in Jerusalem, and in general to claim for Judah priority over the north in religious matters. In an analogous way, Matthew and Luke can be understood as the earliest commentaries on the Gospel of Mark, since they not only add material to Mark's general content, but reorder and in some cases recast that Markan material. The prophetic books also, as we shall see in more detail, are made up of collected traditions associated with a given prophet; and the books in the New Testament bearing the name "John" (Gospel, Epistles, Revelation) may well be materials produced by those who identified closely with the disciple John and who sought to preserve the traditions associated with his proclamation of the faith.

OLD MATERIAL USED IN NEW WAYS

As is clear from all of this, the biblical authors are by no means enslaved to their traditions. As new situations develop, old traditions are used in new and different ways. For example, the same tradition can be interpreted in quite different ways in two biblical writings. The tradition concerning the selection and blessing of Abraham (Gen. 12:1–3; 17:1–8), whose progeny became great and possessed the land of Canaan, is cited both in Ezekiel (Ezek. 33:23–29) and in Isaiah (Isa. 51:1–3), yet for diametrically opposed reasons. While the promise is reaffirmed in Isaiah and is used as the basis for the promise of restoration to Israel, in Ezekiel it is specifically denied and countermanded by God, who through Ezekiel announces that the people may not cite those traditions as a basis for hope and comfort.[3] Again, it is clear from the context in which Mark has placed the saying of Jesus about his true family (Mark 3:31–35) that he means the tradition to cast a negative light on the familial reaction to Jesus: Mark has coupled it with the scribal denunciation of Jesus as demonic (Mark 3:21–35; Mark has inserted the Beelzebul controversy, vv. 23–30, into the story of familial reaction, vv. 21, 31–35). Luke, on the other hand, gives this tradition a positive interpretation by including it in a context that emphasizes the

---

[3] Coats and Long, eds., *Canon and Authority*, 31–32.

need to seek out Jesus and hold fast to him (Luke 8:4–21). In that setting, the fact that mother and brothers seek him out is an example of the correct attitude toward Jesus. The exclusive tone of the saying in Mark (Mark 3:33–34) is transformed into an inclusive tone in Luke (Luke 8:20–21). Similarly, Matthew and Luke have made different use of the parable of the Lost Sheep. In Matthew, as wording and context make clear (Matt. 18:10–17), the point is the need for church members to exert every effort to return an erring fellow Christian to the church, whereas in Luke, wording and context show that that author understood the point to be the need to reach out even to those who in that cultural context would be socially unacceptable. The parable in Luke thus points to the missionary need of the church to reach out to sinners and bring them into the Christian fellowship (Luke 15:1–10, see esp. vv. 2, 10).[4]

It is clear from this that not even the sayings of Jesus were regarded as immutable and unalterable by the authors of the Gospels. Far from having one fixed meaning which remained the same for all time, the sayings of Jesus were evidently regarded as capable of quite different meanings in different situations, and the author who collected those traditions used them to make the theological point he or she thought necessary for those who would read that Gospel. The composition of the Gospels rather clearly proceeds, therefore, along the lines of the collection and interpretation of traditions rather than along the lines of a minutely accurate chronicle of the events of Jesus' life. The purpose is theological rather than chronological or historiographic, as such comparisons of the Gospels with one another make clear.

Again, it is evident that what would on a more rigid view of the nature of the biblical books have to be regarded as discrepancies, and thus as a threat to a view of the Bible as the timeless formulation of unchanging truth, can be explained in a more satisfactory way when one understands that the biblical authors are relying on a variety of traditions as they compose and arrange. On such a view, further, what

---

[4] If, as most scholars agree, one of Luke's sources was Mark, we can speak of Luke's altering the point of the material he took from Mark. In the case of Matthew and Luke, since it appears that neither knew the other's Gospel, it is likely that the parable of the Lost Sheep appeared in their sources with no context and that Matthew and Luke have provided the kind of context each thought best suited to that parable. Although some scholars think the Lukan context is closer to the original, we are not in a position to make any firm judgments.

would under other circumstances appear to be outright contradictions can be understood, if one understands the freedom with which biblical authors could use their traditions, as an interpretative method employed to make a new point in a new situation. Thus, for example, when the author of Psalm 139 feels that the major need is comfort, a tradition of ascent to heaven and descent to Sheol can be used to show the futility, even impossibility, of finding any location that is beyond the sustaining power of God (Ps. 139:8–10). In another context, the prophet Amos is remembered as having used those very same figures to indicate the futility of finding any place that would be out of reach of the punishment of God (Amos 9:2–3). Clearly, to expect a tradition to have one, and only one, meaning wherever it appears is to expect something of the biblical materials that they do not intend to provide.[5]

The dynamic nature of biblical traditions is further demonstrated when Amos can take the tradition of the exodus of Israel, which is the chief example and proof of the love and care of God for Israel (e.g., Deut. 7:7–8), and equate it with the way God rules the fate of other nations, to show that Israel is not immune from her impending doom. Israel can no more point to the land given her as a sign of special divine protection than could the Cushites, the Philistines, or the Arameans (Amos 9:7). Similarly, traditions that remembered the Lord fighting for, and giving victory to, David in his battles against the Philistines are used in another context as evidence that the Lord as holy warrior will fight against Israel and will bring her low. Thus, when there are references in Isaiah 28:21 to the Lord's having arisen at Mount Perazim, where God gave victory over the Philistines (2 Sam. 5:17–20), and to God's rage at the valley of Gibeon, where God also told David how to overcome the same foe (1 Chron. 14:13–16), they are not, as one would expect, assurances that God will again arise to defend Israel and defeat her enemies. Rather, they are cited as examples of the way God will now turn on Israel and deliver her to her enemies.[6]

Such a reversal of traditions does not always render formerly positive judgments negative in intent. In the course of being produced,

---

[5] An excellent study of this mode of employing traditions can be found in W. Brueggemann and H. W. Wolff, *The Vitality of Old Testament Traditions* (Atlanta: John Knox, 1975).

[6] I owe this example to Coats and Long, eds., *Canon and Authority*, 36–37, although it is used there to make a slightly different point.

some prophetic books were edited in such a way that prophetic oracles which clearly pronounced doom on Israel are used to speak of her eventual restoration. Thus, in Hosea, after the prophet's children are named "Not pitied" and "Not my people" to illustrate the fate of Israel (Hos. 1:6–9), a second tradition was introduced, using those same phrases, but this time without the negatives ("You are my people," "You are pitied"), to make just the opposite point. Similarly, an appendix was added to Amos (Amos 9:8b–15), which again promised restoration to Israel by directly contradicting the words that had gone before (compare v. 8a with 8b). Thus, a later editor did with the traditional oracles of Amos what Amos in his turn had done with the traditions of comfort and positive promise he had used. In that way, traditions were used and reused, transformed and retransformed in the process of giving to our biblical books the shape in which we now have them.

This same process occurs in the New Testament as well. A clear example can be found in the way the parable of the Sower is used in various Gospels. Linguistic hints make it rather clear that Mark is responsible for putting it into its present framework in chapter 4, along with other parables and parabolic sayings. The vocabulary of the explanation of the parable (Mark 4:13–20) makes it likely that it arose at a time later than the parable itself, since the explanation is given in missionary vocabulary that developed after Jesus' resurrection and the subsequent ever-widening outreach of Christian proclamation. That explanation, with its emphasis on the fate of the seed in various soils, began a process of turning a parable designed to caution against underestimating the importance of Jesus[7] into a statement about missionary expectations: do not become discouraged if some efforts meet with failure (4:15–19) since the promise of fruitful success is always there and outweighs any failure (v. 20). Luke then uses the parable and explanation as the first of a series of traditions that emphasize the missionary imperative for the church (Luke 8:4–21) and carries out the account of that missionary activity in the second volume of his work, namely, Acts.

Such use of traditions for different purposes than they originally had can be found not only within the Old and New Testaments but

---

[7] On the meaning of the parable, see my *Invitation to Mark* (New York: Doubleday, 1978), 69–70; cf. also my *Mark* in the Proclamation Commentaries series (Philadelphia: Fortress, 1975), 65–69.

also when the Old Testament is used in the New. When Paul, in his effort to show that faith in Christ rather than performance of the law is now the way God wishes human beings to pursue righteousness (Rom. 9:30–10:10), quotes Deuteronomy 30:12–13 in Romans 10:6, he gives it a meaning quite different from that which it bore in its original setting. Instead of using this passage to show, as Deuteronomy did, that superhuman efforts are not necessary in order to fulfill the commands of the law, since it is not some reality remote from the covenant community, Paul uses the passage to justify his claim that it is precisely that performance of the law which the coming of Christ has rendered useless in God's eyes.[8] In using the tradition from the Old Testament with such freedom, Paul is doing nothing different from the way we have seen other biblical authors and compilers using older traditions. That new meanings are found in old traditions, even meanings which were not those originally intended, is a phenomenon that can be observed repeatedly in both Old and New Testaments, as our examples have shown. Thus, when New Testament authors appear to quote an Old Testament text in a form which differs from that which we find in current texts of the Old Testament, or when they discern in a text a meaning other than it may have borne in its original context, they are doing what biblical authors have regularly done in their use of traditions. Far from creating a problem, as such use of texts does for those who want to emphasize an inerrant and hence basically static biblical text, such a practice on the part of New Testament authors simply follows the precedent established by prophets and chroniclers, psalmists and narrators in earlier times. It is one more example of the dynamic nature of traditions in the literature that makes up our Scriptures.

GOD NOT BOUND TO THE PAST

The basic problem being exposed here concerns whether or not God works by means of discontinuity as well as continuity. Put in other terms, it concerns the question as to whether God is a God of the past, and hence bound to the history he has created, or a God of the future,

---

[8] An excellent discussion of this point can be found in C. T. Rhyne, *Faith Establishes the Law* (SBLDS 55; Chico, Calif.: Scholars Press, 1981).

whose future acts can change the significance of history itself. The way in which the prophets used the traditions of the past clearly indicates that they saw God in the latter mode. God is God of the future, and he is free to re-create the meaning of the past by what he does in the future. That constitutes the essential difference between the "true" and the "false" prophets. When Hananiah confronted Jeremiah with the message that God would quickly restore Israel and return what had been pillaged by the Babylonians, Hananiah was simply applying to his time the message of Isaiah: God's wrath will be visited upon his chosen people, but when it passes, God will restore his people (Isa. 9:8 to 12:6). That was the prophetic tradition upon which Hananiah called, and it was precisely that which made him a false prophet. Jeremiah was compelled by the word of God to denounce Hananiah because the traditions upon which Hananiah called were precisely the wrong ones for the new time (see Jer. 28). Evidently a rigid adherence to the form that sacred traditions assumed in the past is precisely the wrong way to honor the word of a God who is living, and who is thus the God of the present and the future as well as of the past.[9]

This same use of traditions characterizes the preaching of Jesus. Not only does he set aside divine commands from the past (e.g., Matt. 5:38; cf. Lev. 24:20), he is also quite willing to contradict them in his words (Mark 10:2–9) as well as in actions he encouraged among his followers (Luke 5:33–38). It was precisely faithfulness to holy traditions of the past that caused Peter to miss the point of a direct word of God to him about what he was permitted to eat, a word that he misunderstood though it was spoken three times (Acts 10:9–17).

In all of this, it is evident that the word of God is a dynamic reality which does new things in new times and which is therefore not bound to the past. That dynamism of the word is clearly evident in the way in which traditions themselves are used in the various books of the Bible. Traditions can be used in new ways, they can be altered, they can be reformulated, even contradicted. It is precisely those figures in the biblical literature who find their certainty in the traditions from the past who with alarming regularity find themselves opposed to the will and word of God.

---

[9] For more on this point, see the work of James Sanders, esp. *Torah and Canon* (Philadelphia: Fortress, 1972), and his essay in Coats and Long, eds., *Canon and Authority.*

The kinds of examples we have given on the preceding pages could be multiplied into the hundreds. It is the recognition of their existence and the meaning they have for the nature of Scripture, and therefore the way we understand it, which lies behind the emergence in the past century of the "critical" view of Scripture.[10] Again, we must be clear that the difference between the conservative view of the nature of Scripture and the critical view is not the difference between the imposition of a prior set of constructs on the text, on the one hand (as conservatives accuse critical scholars of doing), and the willingness to take the text seriously as it presently stands (as conservatives like to claim they do), on the other. Conservatives are quite as willing as critical scholars to construct hypotheses to account for scriptural evidence, and they do it regularly in an effort to defend the prior assumption of inerrancy. Every time a conservative scholar harmonizes discrepancies by appealing to some historic event behind the reports in Scripture, an event which supposedly explains the differences, that scholar is using a construct based on a prior assumption (inerrancy) to account for the present shape of Scripture. It is not a question, as we indicated above, of whether or not a construct is to be permitted to explain the present shape of our Scriptures. It is rather a question of which construct most adequately represents the reality of the Scripture the reader seeks to understand.[11]

ONGOING INTERPRETATION

Viewed in that perspective, it becomes clear that to understand the varied witness in Scripture as the result of continuing attempts to

---

[10] The word *critical* as used in this context does not mean that one is critical of the content of Scripture, but rather that one is critical of one's own prejudices about what the Bible can and cannot mean. Critical scholarship arose in an effort to free interpretation of the Bible from prior understandings of what it could or could not say. The task must obviously still be carried on, and scholars must be critical of their own views as well as of the views of others.

[11] All human understanding involves the construction of hypotheses that enable us to organize and make sense of the phenomena we confront in our daily lives as well as in our scholarly endeavors. In this area, it is the conservative, not the critical, scholar who is open to the charge of imposing a prior category onto the understanding of Scripture (viz., that it is inerrant by modern standards).

fathom God's will for new times is to understand the Bible as the product of a living attempt, never ended, to determine the kind of future into which the God of Israel and of the church is leading his people. To understand Scripture in that way, rather than as a timeless deposit of the will of God that never changes, is to recognize that the task of interpreting God's will for a new time is never finished. It is to realize that the creative period for Scripture is not simply the point of origin, as though God spoke to his people once and then withdrew again into some cloud of unknowing that forever after hid his face. Rather, the creative period of perceiving God's will continues as traditions are interpreted and reinterpreted, as theological reflection on the impact of a holy God on a sinful world struggles to achieve some clarity of expression. As that reflection continues, traditions shift, as we saw, and take on new meanings. Such shifting of tradition can be simply the adaptation of stories to differing environments. When Luke, for example, retells the story of the paralytic brought by friends to Jesus, he describes the roof they dismantle not as the mud roof of the Palestinian house, as in Mark 2:4, but as the roof made of tiles familiar to his own readers (Luke 5:19). Such shifting of traditions, however, can also be as far reaching as the basic recasting of national traditions. For example, the idea of a golden age for Israel during the period of desert wandering, known to Hosea and Jeremiah (Hos. 2:14–15; 11:1–3; Jer. 2:2–3), is lost in the final casting of that tradition and becomes, instead, a period of rebellion and apostasy. Even as they wait at the foot of God's holy mountain, the Israelites profane themselves with an idol (Exod. 32), and that sets the tone for the whole period, an interpretation represented in the New Testament when Stephen, following the lead of Ezekiel, rehearses the history of Israel as one of such apostasy (Acts 7:2–53). Similar major recastings occur when the Mosaic covenant tradition finally achieves ascendancy in our canon over the Davidic covenantal tradition which played so strong a role in the Isaianic prophecies.[12]

All of our biblical texts are therefore the products of interpretation of the will of God as that is illumined in a new time by earlier traditions. Struggling to understand new revelations of God's purpose for them, Israel and the church turn to older traditions to find some clue to how they may cope with such a dynamic God. Our Scriptures

---

[12] On this last point, see esp. Sanders, *Torah and Canon,* 44–45, 56–59.

reflect that process and enshrine that quest. The real threat to a proper understanding of the Bible is therefore to fail to see it in the light of its own origins in this process of interpretation and reinterpretation. To eliminate, through harmonizing and explaining away, the tensions that inevitably result from such struggles to understand God's will for new times is to lose the dynamic witness of the Scriptures to that God. To consider the chief verification of our Gospels some imagined history which one has to reconstruct in order to understand them is to lose the Jesus to whom the Gospels point. The attempts to write a life of Jesus show clearly enough that where historical data are absent and speculation provides it, the result is not the Jesus of history but a Jesus of the pious imagination. What is recovered then is a Jesus as the writer would like him to have been. To consider the chief value of Acts to be a chronicle of the development of the early church, rather than as a theological reflection on what that period had to say for a church which in the author's time was already feeling the stress of division and disunity, is to rob that account of its value for our own similar situation. To harmonize Paul with Acts, in the quest for such a "history," is, as such attempts all too clearly show, to lose Paul as he appears in his letters, with his uncompromising "by faith alone" and his understanding of the radical freedom-responsibility polarity within the Christian faith. To lose the dynamic tensions in the biblical witness, or to want to eliminate them through harmonizing, is thus precisely to lose the witness of Scripture to the dynamic God, who never allows his people to become complacent, or to canonize a holy past.

A further implication of the nature of Scripture as we have outlined it consists in the realization that Scripture has been produced out of the experience of a community as it sought to come to terms with a God whose nature was totally beyond that community's human perceptions, and who therefore acted in ways unaccountable by contemporary social or political customs. Scripture reflects not only God's word to the community but also that community's response, both positive and negative, to that word. Scripture did not drop as a stone from heaven. It grew out of the life of a community chosen by a God the receivers barely understood and often did not want to follow, yet who would not release his people to their own devices. On the other hand, if the community produced Scripture out of its struggle to shape its life to the will of God, that Scripture also sustained the community in times of severe crisis. If one cannot imagine the Bible without the community whose life and struggle of faith it records, one cannot imagine the community without the traditions that helped it understand and sustain itself. The Christian faith, therefore, is not the response to a holy book. Church and Scripture grew up alongside each other—the traditions shaping the life of the church, and the church interpreting and reshaping the traditions in the light of its own proclamation of those traditions. The struggle within the primitive church concerning the question of whether or not a Gentile had first to become a Jew in order to be a Christian is clearly recorded in Paul's letter to the church in Galatia. When the question was resolved, the resolution itself became a part of the Christian tradition and influenced not only further Scripture (that Gentiles do not need first to become Jews is taken for granted in Acts) but even some of the traditions of the sayings and deeds of Jesus (Mark 7 is clearly intended for Gentile readers who are unaware of Jewish customs—vv. 3–4—yet who are expected to read and understand Jesus' words). What the traditions in Galatians portray as unresolved conflict, the later traditions in Mark (and the other Gospels) and Acts portray as further Christian tradition, now resolved in favor of Gentile converts.

In such ways, the form of Scripture that we have is the form used and shaped by the community as it struggled with its own traditions, and whose very struggles in turn were shaped by those same traditions. Scripture is thus the record of the faith and the self-realization of the Christian community as it struggled to understand its own identity and the role God expected it to play in his plan of redemption for a sinful world.

The tensions within Scripture have a further point to make. If the Bible represents the self-understanding of the community that produced it, it is by no means an idealized statement of Christian propaganda. Rather, the Bible, Old and New Testaments alike, is a series of critiques of the very community that produced it. If the New Testament is the product of the church, it is also the church's harshest critic. A cursory reading of the letters of Paul makes clear that they contain a higher proportion of criticism than commendation, and even so irenic a book as Acts betrays that all was not well with the community out of which that book was produced.[13]

---

[13] See, e.g., Acts 6:1; 15:1–2; 16:36–39.

It becomes apparent from all of this that the major significance of the Bible is not that it is a book, but rather that it reflects the life of the community of Israel and the primitive church as those communities sought to come to terms with the central reality that God was present with them in ways that regularly outran their ability to understand or cope. Our understanding of the inspiration of that Scripture must therefore take into account the living reality to which the Bible points. We must take into account the church's affirmation that the Bible is the result of the experience of Israel and of the early church with the God who invaded their world and forced them to come to terms with that fact. In some way or other, our understanding of inspiration must reckon with the interrelation of community and Scripture, as well as with the continuing process of reinterpretation imposed on scriptural traditions by the theological reflections of the communities whose life is mirrored in those writings. We must take seriously Paul's insight that the Spirit is given to the community and that only as members of that community can individuals, themselves bearers of spiritual gifts, enjoy the full range of those gifts (1 Cor. 12).

We have now seen, in brief summary, a sketch of the modern critical view of Scripture and the evidence upon which it is based.[14] We have seen how the evidence presented by Scripture itself, the so-called phenomena, points to an explanation of Scripture as a process in which traditions are formulated and reformulated, interpreted and reinterpreted. This will have a profound effect on the way we understand the inspiration of the writings produced by such a process. To that problem we must now turn.

---

[14] In addition to specific references, I have drawn insight for various points in this chapter from Rahner, *Inspiration in the Bible;* Leander E. Keck, *The Bible in the Pulpit* (Nashville: Abingdon, 1978), esp. ch. 3, "The Bible in the Church"; Leander E. Keck, "The Presence of God Through Scripture" in the *Lexington Theological Quarterly* 10 (1975); John L. MacKenzie, "The Social Character of Inspiration" in *Catholic Biblical Quarterly* 24 (1962); and the work of James Sanders.

Chapter 4

Problems Old and New

Our survey of some attempts to understand the nature of Scripture and its inspiration, and of the nature of Scripture as it has revealed itself through modern critical study, has put us in a position to draw up a kind of balance sheet on the way theories of inspiration can be squared with the nature of the Bible. We may set as a motto over this discussion the statement of a Dutch theologian that "no one of the theories of inspiration is true and good which does not agree with the 'phenomena' of Scripture."[1]

SOME CURRENT EVASIONS

If the liberal understanding of Scripture begins with those phenomena, as we saw, it is in the end also defeated by them. Impressed with the discrepancies and contradictions that can be found within and among the various books in the Bible, the liberal view finally solves the problem of the inspiration of Scripture by denying it any unique inspiration at all. By setting Scripture under the rubric of the total experience of humanity and allowing that totality of knowledge to stand over Scripture as a final court of appeal, the liberal view has abandoned any final sense of Scripture's authority and has equated its inspiration with the "inspiration" of any genius who produces a work of science or art that is out of the ordinary. Confronted with a critical understanding of Scripture, the liberal view has simply abandoned any

---

[1] Berkouwer, *Holy Scripture,* 242.

idea of its unique inspiration; and, impressed with the fact that the Bible bears the marks, the "phenomena," of other books produced by human beings, liberalism finally relegates the Bible to that realm. If speaking of the inspiration of Scripture carries no more meaning than speaking of the inspiration of Shakespeare's *Hamlet* or Beethoven's Ninth Symphony, then such terminology has passed out of the realm of discourse about which we are concerned in this book. Faced with critical discoveries about the nature of the Bible and the problem of inspiration of Scripture, the liberal view solves the problem by denying inspiration.

The conservative scholars, on the other hand, have exercised a different option. Faced with the problems inherent in a critical view of the nature of Scripture and its inspiration, the conservatives have denied the nature of Scripture as critical scholarship has revealed it. Faced with the overwhelming evidence which critical scholarship has uncovered concerning the way in which Scriptures have been composed of traditions that are used and reused, reinterpreted and recombined, conservative scholarship has sought to defend its precritical view of Scripture by imposing that view on Scripture as a prior principle. Unless evidence can be turned or bent to show the inerrancy of Scripture, the evidence is denied (e.g., it did not appear in the errorless autographs). It was precisely the attempt to free studies of the Bible from such dogmatic preconceptions that determined beforehand what Scripture could and could not be allowed to say that fostered the development of critical scholarship in the first place. Critical scholarship is therefore an attempt to allow Scripture itself to tell us what it is, rather than to impose upon Scripture, for whatever worthy motives, a concept of its nature that is not derived from the materials, the "phenomena," found in Scripture itself.[2]

In the attempt to save Scripture from its own "phenomena," conservatives betray their desire to free divine revelation from the limitations of the creaturely and the historical. Yet we never confront God in Scripture except as he speaks within human forms and human history. The word of God in Scripture is not delivered in a timeless and absolute form, unaffected by contemporary cultural and linguistic realities, any more than the Word of God made flesh appeared is so unaffected a form. Indeed, the very thrust of the Bible is that God does

---

[2] On the rise of such critical scholarship, see Berkouwer, *Holy Scripture*, esp. 130–31.

not reveal himself in a timeless fashion, but rather within the swirling realities of human history. If the Christian faith is correct that the final act of God for our redemption occurred in Jesus of Nazareth, then the interpretative key to Scripture lies precisely in the fact that God has become a wholly historical figure in that man. To make of Scripture something more supernatural and timeless than God's own self-revelation in his Son is surely to withdraw oneself from a serious consideration of the intention of Scripture.[3]

That desire to withhold Scripture from the fate of other human writings obscures the nature of Scripture as human testimony in addition to obscuring the witness of Scripture itself to the way God has dealt with, and revealed himself to, human beings. One can get the impression from conservative writings on this problem that in the view of some conservatives God's speaking to us through Scripture deifies those scriptural words by lifting them out of the realm of possible error or discrepancy, not only for the time in which they were written but for all future times as well.

There is, however, in such an assumption, a unique problem seldom if ever broached in conservative writings. If Scripture is in fact free from error in the form in which it transmits divine truth, it must be free from such error not only for the time for which it was written but also for future times in which it will be read. Scripture, therefore, must be recognizably as free from error to the medieval scientist searching for the way to transmute base metal into gold as it must be free from error to the modern physicist seeking a field theory of physical forces, despite the widely differing presuppositions each brings to Scripture about the nature of the physical world. If truth is one, and the Bible as truth must exclude error, on whose presuppositions is that truth to be explained, the alchemist's or the modern physicist's? Whose presuppositions will determine, for example, what is the actual view in the Bible of geography, or geology, or botany, or the process of creation? That this problem is seldom if ever discussed by conservatives points to a naive absolutizing of the current level of scientific theory

---

[3] Again, see the excellent discussion of this point in Berkouwer, *Holy Scripture,* 73–74, 16–17, 28. The point is also well made in the *Constitution on Divine Revelation,* ch. 3, par. 13: "For the words of God, expressed in human language, have been made like human discourse, just as of old the Word of the eternal Father, when he took to Himself the weak flesh of humanity, became like other men."

and knowledge on the part of conservatives. Yet conservative apologetics for the truth of Scripture in all realms of human knowledge are as incapable of dealing with that material on the basis of past presuppositions of human knowledge as they will be on the basis of as yet unformulated presuppositions of human knowledge that only the future will bring. It is as though conservatives assumed that to our time and our time alone the final, unchanging truth of the universe had been revealed. Therein lies the danger in assuming that the Bible really meant to say what we now understand the composition of the physical world to be, in such areas as creation, the flood, and other physical phenomena. The need for apologetics for a particular world view and the idea of truth as unchangeable from age to age make the task of conservative apologetics for scriptural inerrancy a uniquely unprofitable one.

Further symptoms of the problem of desiring to exclude Scripture from the realm of other human writings surface when conservative writers attribute to Christ, despite his own explicit denial, omniscience in all matters religious, scientific, and historical, and when these writers are moved to propose that God allowed the autographs of Scripture to perish lest they be a temptation to idolatry.[4] The fact that adoration of Scripture can be imagined as a religious problem points to a basic difficulty with the conservative view of the Bible.

Yet another difficulty with such a view becomes evident when conservatives see the major thrust of the Bible to be the enunciation of doctrine, or "teaching." It is simply assumed that until one has found the "teaching" intended in some portion of Scripture, one has not yet understood it. That psalms are designed to awaken our reverence for the God whose praises are there sung or that other parts of Scripture contain the simple outpourings of gratitude and supplication that accompany a lively sense of the reality and the presence of God in his world is distorted or simply denied by such a view of Scripture. Yet if Scripture is a divine instrument of revelation sent by the ultimate authorship of God, there is no room for such merely human components.[5] The result of such a view is the tendency to

---

[4] I have in mind specifically Harold Lindsell.

[5] A further difficulty is provided for this view when a biblical author (Paul) avers that he is unsure of his facts (1 Cor. 1:16) or explicitly denies that what he is saying comes from the Lord (1 Cor. 7:25).

understand revelation in the form of timeless propositions and hence to withdraw it from as much significant human contact and contamination as possible.

That such a view of Scripture renders difficult the reception and proclamation of the message of that Scripture is coming to be recognized by some who count themselves as belonging to the conservative approach to Scripture. To make inerrancy the touchstone of all truth, so that those who deny inerrancy in its last detail cannot be trusted to speak any scriptural truth, is simply self-defeating. Such a fixation on errorlessness has hindered effective Bible study in the view of other conservatives.[6] The upshot of such suggestions has been a struggle over who has the right to the term *evangelical,* a term that die-hard inerrantists seek to deny to those who begin to question the usefulness of such a wooden view of inerrancy imposed on Scripture. Yet to the suggestion that verbal inspiration is incompatible with modern critical scholarship only if verbal inspiration is equated with errorlessness in every detail,[7] the recently formed International Council on Biblical Inerrancy answers that "the authority of Scripture is inescapably impaired if this total divine inerrancy is *in any way* limited or disregarded" (italics mine).[8]

It is clear, therefore, that some conservative scholars, confronted with a critical view of Scripture that threatens the basis of their theories of inspiration, have chosen to ignore or deny the critical view of Scripture. As the liberals solved the problem by denying the unique inspiration of Scripture, these conservatives solve the problem by denying the nature of Scripture.[9]

There is, of course, a third option, and it is the one that has been chosen by the vast majority of biblical scholars who are not conservatives. That option is simply to say nothing about the problem at all. Aware that most views of inspiration that claim for Scripture some

---

[6] E.g., Rogers, ed., *Biblical Authority,* 68, 122. The whole volume of essays is well worth careful reading.

[7] A suggestion of Barr, *Fundamentalism,* 287.

[8] "A Short Statement," par. 5. This is of course not in direct response to Professor Barr, but makes clear what that direct answer would be.

[9] Here, as earlier, I have devoted more space to the conservative than to the liberal views, simply because the conservatives at least have continued to speak of the inspiration of Scripture in a way that points to the unique authority of the Bible. For that reason, I take their views more seriously than I do those of the liberals and so feel it necessary to deal with them in more detail.

unique authority are incompatible with the view of Scripture with which they work, critical scholars have opted for silence on the problem.[10] Where they have dealt with it in the classroom, it has tended to be in traditional forms that could not stand close scrutiny as to their compatibility with the view of Scripture used by such scholars when they do their work of exegesis and interpretation. When that incompatibility rises to the level of consciousness, the tendency is simply to avoid any talk of inspiration except perhaps the most general kind of affirmation.

INADEQUACY OF THE PROPHETIC MODEL

Underlying all of the reticence of critical scholars to speak about the inspiration of Scripture is, one suspects, an intuitive awareness that the prophetic model of inspiration, though it is maintained by those conservatives and liberals alike who still speak and write about inspiration, simply is no longer capable of bearing the weight it once carried.[11] When people think of the "inspiration of Scripture," one suspects, the mental image still pictures isolated authors who produced (either by writing or by dictation) Scripture out of their own heads. If sources were involved (and there is now almost universal agreement that at least some sources were used in at least some of the books of the Bible), those sources also were digested by that one author, who then produced the book essentially as we now have it.[12] It is that mental image, we want to argue, which a modern, critical understanding of the way Scripture came into being has rendered

---

[10] When Rahner, *Inspiration in the Bible*, 6, observes that "on the average, Roman Catholic Scripture scholars, although by no means denying or doubting the inspiration of the Bible, prefer not to touch it at all in their exegetical work," he speaks about most Protestant Scripture scholars as well.

[11] Abraham (*Divine Inspiration*, 44) points out that such a way of understanding inspiration inevitably puts major emphasis on God's "speaking" to the prophet, and with it then comes the notion of God's "dictating" the content of Scripture (see also pp. 36–37). It is the confusion of the idea of "speaking" and "dictation" with the idea of "inspiration" that Abraham finds a major unnoticed presupposition, and hence difficulty, for any inerrantist view. He argues if dictation is abandoned, "the commitment to inerrancy must go as well" (p. 34).

[12] See Vawter, *Biblical Inspiration*, 114.

obsolete. A catalog of the problems associated with the model of inspiration constructed on the prophetic image (i.e., a person, inspired of God, then writes or causes to be written a book of Scripture, as in Jer. 36:1–2) will help to clarify that point. All of them center around the idea that each book of Scripture has an author.

A major and widely acknowledged problem, at least among critical scholars, centers around our inability to identify most of the authors of the biblical books. That has long since rendered obsolete the claim that Scripture is inspired because it was written by identifiably inspired persons, i.e., prophets in the case of the Old Testament, apostles in the case of the New. The insistence that Moses wrote the Pentateuch and that Paul wrote every letter bearing his name grows out of that affirmation. Most critical scholars would agree, however, that, in the shape we have them, most books of the Bible cannot be associated with a single individual, least of all with a single individual whose identity we can clearly establish.[13] While some books of the Bible do bear the names of one individual (e.g., some of the New Testament epistles), others bear the names of several persons as authors (e.g., 1 and 2 Cor., Phil., 1 and 2 Thess.), while a great many more are simply anonymous (e.g., the Torah, the Gospels). If, therefore, any theory of inspiration is to be persuasive, it cannot be predicated on the identity or roles of the persons who were the authors of the various canonical books of Scripture, since sure knowledge of them not only is not available, but, to judge from many of the books themselves, would not even be useful. Without exception, the authors of the Gospels did not think their own identity important enough even to mention. Where Scripture is silent, speculation, however pious, can do little to clarify the issue, and it is precisely in such speculation that preconceived notions about Scripture are most likely to surface.

A second problem associated with the prophetic model for the inspiration of the books of the Bible lies in the question of the inspiration of the author's intention. If statistics are confused, or facts are erroneous, can we say that while all of the written material may not be inspired, the point that the author wants to make carries the burden of inspiration? Aside from the fact that such an intention again implies an individual author who had a deliberate intention to

---

[13] See MacKenzie, "The Social Character of Inspiration," 115.

be conveyed by what he or she wrote, the question emerges about the value of that intention if it must be reinterpreted for us to be able to appropriate it. For example, if, as seems clear, the first chapter of Genesis, written within the framework of divine legislation, intended to ground the liturgical aspects of that law upon the very act of divine creation, it clearly needed to see creation in terms of seven actual days, so that the special observance of the seventh day, the Sabbath, could be justified. What then happens to the inspired intention if we are compelled to find it in the broader assertion that God is the source and sustainer of created reality because we can no longer accept creation as having taken place in a week's time? If the author who wrote Genesis 6:1–4 took over a myth widespread in the ancient world about the intermarriage of gods and human beings, albeit to make a nonmythological point, yet believed he or she was reporting solid fact with that "myth," what happens to the intention of that author if we disagree on the factuality of the illustration? To be sure, truth can be illustrated by fiction as well as by fact, but if the author intended to report fact and we understand it as myth, what has happened to the inspired intention? Is our nonmythological understanding commensurate with our author's actual intention?[14] The appeal to the intention of the inspired individual who wrote a biblical book is thus also rendered problematic, even on the assumption that there was an individual author. What happens when, in addition, the very production by such an individual author is called into question?

Far more significantly, however, modern critical study of the Bible has questioned, at least by implication, whether individual authors, in any useful meaning of such words, can be appealed to when speaking of the books of the Bible. For example, New Testament scholars have long since recognized that our first three Gospels, and to a somewhat lesser extent the fourth as well, consist for the most part of traditions that had an extended oral existence before they were incorporated into our Gospels. If such material was told and retold, and, as with all oral tradition, was in a sense "composed" each time it was retold, the importance of the person who finally assembled that material is reduced in considerable measure. If, in addition, many of those traditions were put into their present arrangement before the

---

[14] I owe the example of Gen. 6:1–4 to Vawter, *Biblical Inspiration,* 131.

"author" finally set them down, then that author's significance is reduced yet more. If the one who wrote down such material did little else than reduce to writing what already had long circulation and acceptance in oral form, how significant is it to locate inspiration in that act of "writing down"? Does it not much rather lie in the composition of that material? Yet it is beyond our ability to identify the origin of such composition, and, as is the case with oral traditions in ancient groups, the material may not owe its present form to any one identifiable, inspired individual. Oral traditions are combined and recombined, and adapted to the situation into which they are spoken.

It has also become apparent that much of this material in both Old and New Testaments was assembled to serve functions within the religious community. The material was inspired by the community's experience, was told for the benefit of the community, and hence owed its origin more to a communal than to an individual experience. As this material is handed on from generation to generation, especially in the case of the Old Testament, and is adapted and re-created to meet new situations, the "creation" of that material ceases altogether to become the act of one inspired individual. Indeed, the actual writing down of such material, while certainly done by an individual, may actually be the least important aspect of its production as "inspired" literature.

In addition to all of that, it is also apparent that once such material was written down, it was worked and reworked in its written form, so that even where we have an inspired individual, such as a prophet, standing at the origin of a form of community tradition, the final writing of that tradition is perhaps the least important aspect of its preservation. Much that we have from Jeremiah has been preserved only from Deuteronomistic perspective. The psalms bear evidence of several editions and much reworking, both individually and as smaller collections, before they were assembled into their present shape. Who is the "inspired" individual? The first author, whose work has since been substantially recast? The one who recast material he or she did not in fact originate? The person or persons who assembled material they neither composed nor recast into our present canonical collection?[15]

---

[15] I have drawn both ideas and examples for this discussion from Barr, *Fundamentalism,* 156; MacKenzie, "The Social Character of Inspiration," 116–21; Vawter, *Biblical Inspiration,* 2, 93, 106–7, 130–31.

The same problem arises when we consider the interrelationship of the Gospels. If Matthew or Luke takes material from Mark and recasts it, which is the inspired form, that given to it originally in the Markan composition, or the recast form it assumes in Luke or Matthew? And if, in addition, Mark is also recording a tradition known from oral or written tradition, and has recorded it without change, as he evidently did on occasion, where are we to locate the inspiration for that material? If, as further seems likely, that pre-Markan tradition had achieved its present form through its use and reuse in the worship life of the Christian community, does the originator of that form of the tradition, whoever he or she may have been, have any contribution of significance to make to the process, especially if the ultimate origin of the substance was a word or act of Jesus himself? And if, finally, Mark preserved a number of traditions simply so that they would not be lost, then his contribution to that material, in the sense of inspiration, has diminished to the vanishing point. Can the inspiration of the material rest on the individual who made no contribution to the material other than to write it down, as is the case with our Gospel authors in some instances?

All of this ought to make it clear that our contemporary understanding of the origins of our Scripture, Old and New Testaments alike, has rendered obsolete the model of inspiration which understands the production of each biblical book to be the result of the inspired work of an inspired author. It is that fact, more than any other critical view or conclusion, that calls into question the usual view of inspiration. The theological stance, therefore, whether conservative or liberal, of the person who understands inspiration on the prophetic model is thus no longer an issue. Both conservatives and liberals alike have tended, without further reflection, to understand inspiration of Scripture on the model of the prophetic image. An author, inspired by God, sets down God's word for the people. It is that model, as we have seen, which modern understandings of the nature of Scripture have rendered nugatory.

The task before us, therefore, is to identify the locus of the inspiration of Scripture in the light of the findings of modern critical study. If we can describe that locus in such a way that we are not forced to abandon the final authority of Scripture, we will be able to avoid the problem inherent in the liberal understanding of inspiration, where such authority is lost. On the other hand, we must not let our desire to preserve the authority of Scripture cause us to deny the discoveries of the past century and more about the nature of Scripture and the processes by which it has been composed and assembled. In that way, we must seek to avoid the problems inherent in the conservative understanding of inspiration. Finally, we must seek to understand inspiration in such a way that it is not dependent on the model of the prophet, to whom God speaks a word and who then writes that down or causes his words to be written for contemporary and future generations. Constructing such a model for understanding the inspiration of Scripture is not a simple task, and hence a simple solution may not be appropriate, even if it were desirable. Yet complexity must not deter us from the attempt, and it is that attempt, and its ramifications, that must occupy us in the remaining pages of this book.

Chapter 5

The Inspiration of Scripture: A Proposal

It is our task in the following pages to inquire about the nature of the inspiration of Holy Scripture, taking into account the discoveries about the nature of those Scriptures which have been made during the past century by the use of critical methods of study. We look upon such critical studies not as an obstacle to be surmounted, nor even as a development to be regretted, but rather as an opportunity to see the Scriptures for what they really are. It is precisely the human dimension in Scripture that has made such critical studies not only fruitful but necessary, and any view of the inspiration of such Scripture will have to take the human dimension with utmost seriousness if it itself intends to be taken seriously.[1] The task of understanding the inspiration of Scripture is thus the task of asking how we can claim for a very human literature the unique authority of God.

Our first step will be to examine three key elements that must be taken into account in any attempt to understand the inspiration of Scripture. Those three are: the witness of Scripture itself to its own

---

[1] As Vawter, *Biblical Inspiration,* 86, has pointed out, such historical and literary-critical approaches to the biblical literature were not imposed on the Bible as alien disciplines developed from secular models. Rather, most modern literary and historical-critical methods employed on nonbiblical literature today received their impetus and original forms from the study of Scripture. Critical studies were developed not from skepticism about the Bible's message, but rather from a desire to take with utmost seriousness the nature of the biblical witness and the kind of literature in which it was embedded.

nature, the close relationship between community and Scripture, and the importance of the formation of the canon for understanding the formation of inspired Scripture. Each of these elements will provide necessary information for understanding the inspiration of our Bible. First, then, the witness of Scripture to itself.

WHAT THE BIBLE SAYS ABOUT ITSELF

As has often been observed, it is remarkable how little Scripture has to say about itself and about the process by which it was formed. It has even less to say about its nature as inspired. One gets the impression from Scripture that its chief task is to point away from itself to something or someone who is far more important,[2] and we will want to examine that phenomenon below. There are one or two passages which do speak of Scripture and which have been used by those who want to speak seriously of the inspiration of Scripture. We must examine those passages carefully, to see what it is they say, and what they do not say. The passage that comes first to mind in such a connection is 2 Timothy 3:16.

The more immediate context of this verse is 2 Timothy 3:10 to 4:5, a unit concerning Timothy, to whom the letter is addressed.[3] The section begins with an indication that persecution and end times go together, which puts the present threat of persecution in its proper perspective, namely, that with the dawning of the last times, persecutions can be expected and must be borne. Yet as Christ delivered Paul from his persecutions, so all good people will similarly be persecuted but also (by implication) delivered. In such times, Timothy is to be strong in his own faith, remembering what he has known of that faith since childhood and also remembering the good teachers he has had. The sacred writings from which he learned the faith as a child will continue to sustain his faith, since such Scriptures are inspired by God and hence are useful for teaching, reproof, correction, and continuing

---

[2] The anonymity of the Gospels is an example of the way the biblical literature points away from itself to its content.

[3] Whether or not Paul wrote this letter has no bearing on this point. Because of vocabulary and style, many scholars feel it was written by a follower of Paul rather than by Paul himself, but that question will not affect our purpose of determining the scope and intention of 2 Tim. 3:16.

training in righteousness. They will aid devout persons in maintaining their faith so that they can continue in the Christian life. So equipped, Timothy is to get on with his task of evangelizing.

The key verse, 3:16, will admit of two possible translations. It could be understood either as "All scripture [or every Scripture] is inspired and profitable," or "All inspired scripture [or every inspired Scripture] is also profitable." The first translation assumes that the adjective "inspired" is in the predicate position and would be parallel to a similar construction in 1 Timothy 4:4 ("because every creation of God is good"). The second translation assumes that the adjective "inspired" is in the attributive position ("inspired Scripture") and would be parallel in structure and meaning to the phrase "sacred writings" in the verse immediately preceding (v. 15). There is no sure way to determine whether the author of this verse wanted to stress that every Scripture is *both* inspired *and* useful for teaching, and the like, or whether he wanted to stress that *inspired* Scripture is useful in that way. The very ambiguity of the language, however, makes one wonder whether the author really intended to make a statement about the inspiration of Scripture at all. It is more likely that the intention is to emphasize the continuing utility of Scripture for religious purposes, even after one has learned the rudiments of the faith from it, a point the context also supports.

The vocabulary of the verse is also instructive. That our author is thinking of the Old Testament is clear both from the language of v. 15, where the Greek for "sacred writings," *hiera grammata,* is the term used for those writings common among Greek-speaking Jews (see Philo, *Life of Moses* 2.292; Josephus, *Antiquities* 10.210), and from the fact that at the time of writing, there was as yet no New Testament. The word for "inspired," *theopneustos* (literally, "Godbreathed"), is used only here in the New Testament, but appears four times in pre-Christian Greek literature, and again accurately reflects the way Jews of the first century viewed Scripture.[4] Whatever the author of this verse intended to say, therefore, he said with reference to what we now call the Old Testament, which was of course the only Scripture the primitive church possessed.

Clearly, however, the verse is not intended to be a statement about the inspiration of the Old Testament, either. The point of the verse is not

---

[4] See J. N. D. Kelly, *A Commentary on the Pastoral Epistles* (BNTC 14; Peabody, Mass.: Hendrickson, 1964), 203; cf. also Vawter, *Biblical Inspiration,* 8–11.

the nature of Scripture in itself, but the nature of Scripture *for the purpose of aiding the Christian life.* The point of 2 Timothy 3:15–17 lies in the emphasis that Scriptures can sustain, as they can also train, Christians in their faith. Such instruction has come to Timothy from people (v. 14) as well as from Scripture (v. 15); and that Scripture is also suitable for continuing training, not just for original instruction. Such Scriptures have the ability to make one "wise unto salvation through faith in Jesus Christ," as they have the intention of "equipping the man of God for every good work."[5] If the author thought inspiration made Scriptures infallible in anything, it was clearly in such religious matters as teaching, reproof, correction, and training in righteousness. They are intended to make one wise unto salvation, not unto matters of botany, biology, history, or geology.[6] There is no hint here that Scripture has anything other than a strictly religious point. Its intention is to provide the kind of information that will aid one in finding salvation through faith in Christ. Typically, this passage points not to itself but to something else, in this case the Christian life; thus it shows that its essential nature consists in witness to a reality beyond itself.[7] Such information as it provides is aimed at gaining obedience to God's revelation of himself in his Son.

If the nature of Scripture is secondary to the central intention of these verses, however, it is nevertheless true that the author thinks Scripture has a central role to play both in the salvation of Timothy and in his task of proclaiming that salvation to others (2 Tim. 4:1–5). For that task, Scripture is important—indeed, along with other teaching, it is sufficient and indispensable. Clearly, for this author, the Scriptures of the Old Testament have a central role to play in the drama of Christian proclamation.

A second passage often cited in a discussion of the inspiration of Scripture is 2 Peter 1:20–21.[8] The more immediate context in this case has to do with false prophets who can divide the Christian community (cf. 2 Pet. 2:1–3). The broader context concerns the question about

---

[5] Translations by author.

[6] On this point, see Berkouwer, *Holy Scripture,* 140; Orr, *Revelation and Inspiration,* 160–62; Davis, *Debate About the Bible,* 38.

[7] See Berkouwer, *Holy Scripture,* 183.

[8] Again, there is wide agreement among critical scholars that the disciple Peter did not write this epistle. Whether or not that is the case, it will not affect the attempt to elicit the intended meaning of 2 Pet. 1:20–21.

whether Christ in fact will return (cf. 3:2–10; the appearance of the Greek *parousia* in 1:16). The gist of the passage (1:16 to 2:3) within which our verses occur concerns the contrast between certainty about the fulfillment of prophecies about the Lord's return based on the event of the Transfiguration and uncertainty about that return based on "cleverly devised myths" (1:16) and false interpretation of those prophecies (1:20–21).

There are some problems in interpreting the intended meaning of the text. One such problem concerns the phrase "made more sure" (RSV) in 1:19. The comparative form of the adjective could be translated: "We have the prophetic word as a surer thing," i.e., surer than the Transfiguration event, an advantage since they know of the Transfiguration only at second hand, but can read the prophetic word themselves. On the other hand, the author may want to say that his readers may trust the prophecies now that their proleptic fulfillment in the Transfiguration has made them all the surer.

A second, and potentially more important, problem occurs in v. 20. As the RSV translates the verse, it is clear that what is at issue is an individual's private interpretation of prophecy, something inadmissible since prophecy did not come at private initiative. Since God moved the prophets to speak, the implication seems to be, God must also interpret the prophecies, as apparently the author thinks God did in the Transfiguration. The Greek will also bear another meaning, however. This second meaning would relate prophetic interpretation in v. 20 not to the one who reads prophecy, but to the prophet himself. That is, v. 20 would intend to say that the prophetic interpretation of various events Israel experienced in its history was due not to the prophet's own ideas but to ideas given to him by God. If Amos, for example, spoke of the doom of Israel, it was not because he somehow thought up that interpretation of present and future events by himself, but rather because he was moved to understand events in that way by God's own Spirit. On that analogy, the flow of thought in 2 Peter 1:20–21 would be: no prophecy is due to the prophet's own thoughts or reflections, since prophecy does not come by human impulse but rather by the movement of God's own Spirit.[9] The import of that for

---

[9] The Greek of 2 Pet. 1:20–21 would be translated this way: "You must first of all be aware of this, that no prophecy of Scripture comes by way of personal

the author's argument is clear: prophecies are surer than cleverly devised myths because they are based on God's own Spirit, while (by implication) the myths are due to human impulse. The verses thus become a statement about the origin of prophecy rather than about the way prophecies are to be interpreted. Since the passage says nothing about the correct interpretation of prophecies but is intended to assure the readers that prophecies are sure and trustworthy, this second interpretation would seem more likely to be the correct one.

Such a view is supported by an almost exact paraphrase of these verses in Philo and by the thrust of the opening paragraph of 1 Peter. Writing in *Who Is the Heir of Divine Things?* Philo remarks: "For a prophet has no utterance of his own, but all his utterance came from elsewhere, the echoes of another's voice."[10] This is a close parallel to what we have suggested is the intention of 2 Peter 1:20–21. A similar view of prophecy is reflected in 1 Peter 1:10–12, where that author makes clear that the impulse to speak was provided to the prophets by "Christ's spirit within them" (author's translation), which prompted them to announce beforehand the sufferings of Christ. Again, what the prophets said was not their own but was given them by the Spirit. While we would not want to argue that the author of 2 Peter deliberately paraphrased Philo, he may have been influenced by the statement in 1 Peter, and the view expressed by Philo may well have been current in the circles within which the author of 2 Peter moved.

However those questions be resolved, it is clear that the passage in 2 Peter has little to say directly about the inspiration of Scripture. It is equally clear, however, that the passage intends to have the readers take Old Testament prophecy seriously as coming not from the prophets themselves, but rather from the impulse of God's Spirit. Again, for our author, Scripture is to be taken seriously, and it plays a key role in the understanding of the Christian faith. A third passage, the last we shall consider, that speaks of the authority of Scriptures is John 10:35. The context is Jesus' attendance in Jerusalem at the Feast of Dedication. Challenged to declare whether he is the Christ, Jesus points to

---

interpretation, because no prophecy ever came by human will, but rather men being moved by the Holy Spirit spoke from God."

[10] *Who Is the Heir?* 259 (trans. Colson). Philo was a first-century Jewish scholar who attempted to combine Greek philosophical insights with Old Testament materials as an apologetic for Judaism.

his works, and concludes that he and the Father are one. Moved to stone him, the Jews are asked by Jesus for what good work of his they do this. They reply, not for his works, but for his blasphemy in making himself, a man, into God. Jesus points to Psalm 82:6, where God, addressing the heavenly court, refers to the judges of Israel as "gods," albeit in a negative context (despite that fact, they shall die). Jesus says that if they could be called gods, he who is greater than they can hardly be charged with blasphemy if he calls himself God's Son.

Within the context of that passage, Jesus, after quoting from the psalm, which he refers to as "your [i.e., the Jews'] law," remarks that "Scripture cannot be deprived of its validity" (a more accurate rendering of John 10:35b than the RSV: "Scripture cannot be broken"). The intention of that remark is to strengthen Jesus' argument by citing a passage from the Old Testament that Jews of his time regarded as binding. Since that Scripture is true, Jesus implies, you cannot ignore it. Hence, in rejecting Jesus' claims, they are also involved in rejecting their own "law," something that they know they are not to do. The point is to underline the irrefutability of Jesus' argument, since it is drawn from their own Scriptures.

Of the three, John 10:35 says the least about the nature of Scripture or its inspiration. Jesus simply recalls to his Jewish opponents something they all believed, i.e., that their Scriptures could not be nullified if they intended to remain faithful to God. While Jesus is remembered as sharing such a high view of the law (e.g., Matt. 5:17–18), his failure to require his followers to abide by it (e.g., Matt. 9:14–17; 12:1–8) was a continuing source of conflict with those Jews who observed it strictly. In that larger context, the reference to the law as not being capable of being nullified is best understood as a method employed in the Johannine story to point to the self-contradictory nature of the accusation from Jesus' Jewish opponents.

Taken together, however, these three passages do point to an assumption that God is the ultimate source of the Old Testament Scriptures, and for that reason they are to be taken seriously. It is equally clear that there is nothing in these passages about verbal inerrancy or errorlessness in matters of secular interest. The focus is on the religious intent of Scriptures: they point to Christ and make wise unto salvation through faith in him. Only if inerrancy is brought to the text as a presupposition can any kind of support be found for it in these passages. That inference is not grounded exegetically.

The same conclusion can be drawn about the more general view of Scripture reflected in both Old and New Testaments. That God is the ultimate source of Scripture is clear when the prophets attribute their words and deeds to him (e.g., Exod. 4:30; 7:1–2; Deut. 31:19, 22; 2 Sam. 23:2; 1 Kgs. 22:14; Isa. 8:1; Jer. 1:9; 36:1–2; Ezek. 2:7; Hos. 1:2; Amos 1:3, 6, 9; Hab. 2:2), or when New Testament authors claim that their words and deeds come from God (e.g., John 10:25; 12:49; Heb. 3:7; 4:7–8; 1 Cor. 2:13; 1 Thess. 2:13).[11] The constant appeal by New Testament authors to the Old Testament to confirm the points they make shows the high veneration they gave to those writings. Similarly, the writings of our New Testament regularly assume their own authoritative character which, in the context of the faith within which they were created, can only mean an authority derived from God himself (e.g., 1 Cor. 2:4–10; 14:37–38; Gal. 1:11–12; 1 Thess. 1:5; 2:13; 1 John 4:6; Rev. 22:19).

While the New Testament authors shared with their Jewish contemporaries a high reverence for the Old Testament writings as having their source in the will and words of God, they did not feel themselves bound to them in any literal sense. Jesus' willingness to rephrase or even contradict scriptural commands (e.g., Matt. 5:21–45; Mark 10:2–9), his willingness to ignore parts of the law (e.g., Mark 7:14–19) or allow his followers to do so (e.g., Luke 6:1–5); Paul's willingness to play one passage of the Old Testament against another (e.g., Gal. 3:11–12), along with the freedom with which quotations from the Old Testament are adapted to suit better the argument they are employed to buttress, all point to an almost sovereign disregard of the actual letter of that Scripture. Clearly, what they regarded highly was the message, not the letter of that literature, and, above all, they prized its character as a witness to Christ.

Once it is realized that the Old Testament was highly regarded by New Testament authors as a divinely inspired witness to the coming and significance of Christ, the way those Scriptures are used becomes clear and consistent. Because that witness is true, it is clear that God stands behind it, and thus its inspiration can be assumed without question. Where the Old Testament witness to Christ is less clear than might be desired, it can be clarified by rephrasing to make the witness more clear. Where the actual event of which the New Testament speaks outran the

---

[11] I owe many of these references to Davis, *Debate About the Bible,* 54–55.

statements in the Old Testament, those Old Testament statements could be ignored or even contradicted. The value of Scripture therefore lay in its witness to the coming and the meaning of Jesus as Christ, not in anything it told about history or geology or any other such subjects. Similarly, the New Testament Scriptures see themselves as witnesses to that same event, a view encapsulated by Paul when he announced that his goal was simply to proclaim Christ as Lord, and to be nothing more than a servant to that goal (2 Cor. 4:5). The New Testament authors apparently intended their writings to function as they also assumed the Old Testament writings did: as a witness to God's act of redemption in his Son. We would do those New Testament authors as much of a disservice in finding the importance of their works in some kind of inerrancy which took all our efforts to defend as we would in disregarding their understanding of the nature of the Old Testament and seeking to find there a literal inerrancy as well. Scripture itself apparently thinks it can be inspired as witness to God's saving deeds without having to be regarded as inerrant in matters not central to that witness.[12]

SCRIPTURE AND THE COMMUNITY OF FAITH

The second of the three key elements to be investigated, along with the witness of Scripture to its own inspiration, and the way in which the canon was formed, is the nature of the relationship between Scripture and the community out of which it grew and for which it was written.

Our earlier discussion of the use of traditions by the spokesmen and spokeswomen of God in Scripture made clear that it is precisely the traditions of the community that provide the context within which those Scriptures are produced. Indeed, it would appear that it is precisely the context of the community and its traditions that give meaning to the personal experiences of those in the Bible who speak for God. That is true even when the spokesperson is led to oppose practices within the community and to use earlier traditions to make a point directly opposed to the point those earlier traditions had sought to make. Thus, for

---

[12] For a good discussion of the nature of Scripture as witness, see Berkouwer, *Holy Scripture*, 164–66.

example, the prophets are able to use the traditions about God's giving the Promised Land to Israel, as he had promised to the fathers, not as a guarantee that as God's promise is sure, so the possession of the land is sure. Rather, the prophets use the traditions as a threat that just as God gave the land, so he can take it away again if Israel proves to be disobedient and rebellious against that God. In both instances, however, the context within which the future of the chosen people was understood was the context of the community and the traditions which gave meaning to that community. The spokesperson for God draws on the faith and traditions of the community to which the word of God is to be spoken. We will form the clearest picture of the originators of Scripture if we understand them not as individuals who have gotten their message independently of any other cultural or social forces—as "outsiders," as it were, come to say something totally new to a group as strange to the originator as he to them—but rather as members of a community which draws the meaning of its existence from the traditions that the spokespersons are also employing to understand and communicate God's message to those people. Spokespersons and Scripture are thus intimately involved in the life and in the tradition-based self-understanding of that community.

Much of what we have in Scripture is the written sedimentation of the historic experiences of that community and the resulting understanding of itself and its meaning within God's plan. Thus, as recent Old Testament research has shown, the Hexateuch (the first six books of the Old Testament) represents the narrative expression of the central confession of faith of the community whose story the Hexateuch tells. That confession finds expression in succinct form in Joshua 24:2–13; 1 Samuel 12:8; and Deuteronomy 6:21–23; 26:5–9, and is sung in Psalms 105–106; 135; and 136, and represents the interpretative key that must be brought to the narratives in the Hexateuch even when theological points seem to be absent from the text. The Hexateuch is therefore at heart not so much history as confession of faith of a community that understood its history as the working out of the purposes of God to which it pointed in its confession. Thus, Scripture and community develop together and cannot be understood apart from each other.[13]

---

[13] For an excellent discussion of this point, see Sanders, *Torah and Canon;* I drew this example from pp. 16–20.

Similarly, though the prophets represent trenchant critiques of the social and religious practices of Israel, they nevertheless arise from within that community and can be understood only as having their roots in the same purposes of God and the confessions of faith in that purpose as do the more positively oriented recitals of history contained in the Old Testament. It is a truism to note that apart from the community there would have been no prophets, but it is nevertheless an accurate insight into the relationship of the prophetic literature to the community to which it was addressed. The prophets are trying to recall that community to a way of life more consonant with its origins and its confessions of faith. Indeed, what binds the two—critique and recital—together within the same community of faith, and hence within the same body of Scripture, is the intention of each to keep the community conformed to the purposes of God enunciated in those confessions.

The New Testament also embodies the same struggle within the community of faith for a more faithful expression in its life and theology of the traditions that tell of its origin and purpose. It is evident that that is what Paul tried to do in his epistles. It is also clear, as recent research has begun to make apparent, that even the narrative portions of the New Testament, the Gospels, and Acts also have as their purpose the admonition and correction of the community whose traditions they use and whose history they recite. The different ways in which each of the Gospels shapes and presents the traditions of the words and deeds of Jesus appear to be due to the needs faced by the community to which each Gospel was directed, and from whose life each Gospel emerged.[14]

If it is true, therefore, that the church, by its production of Scripture, created materials which stood over it in judgment and admonition, then it is also true that Scripture would not have existed

---

[14] The method of "redaction criticism," in which Gospels are compared with one another in careful and detailed study, has opened this new way of understanding the more specific purpose of each Gospel. Such an understanding is then made the explicit object of study in the method of "narrative criticism," which seeks to show the unique elements of character and plot, among other elements, within each Gospel. A convenient introduction to the results of such study can be found in the volumes treating the Gospels in the Proclamation Commentaries published by Fortress Press.

save for the community and its faith out of which Scripture grew. That means that church and Scripture are joint effects of the working out of the event of Christ. The close tie between community and Scripture has a most important consequence for our thinking about the inspiration of that Scripture. It is this: if Scripture is to be understood as inspired, then that inspiration will have to be understood equally in terms of the community that produced those Scriptures. Inspiration, in short, occurs within the community of faith and must be located at least as much within that community as with an individual author.

In fact, an understanding of the close relationship between community and Scripture will aid us in overcoming a major hurdle to understanding the nature of scriptural inspiration: the hurdle, namely, of thinking that scriptural books are inspired because they were composed by inspired authors. As we saw, biblical "authors" or compilers regularly used traditions that had been formulated prior to the composition of the book in which they came to be included. As we also saw, that fact makes it all but impossible to understand that such materials can have been inspired only when they appeared in the final context in which we now have them, an understanding that the prophetic model of the inspired author writing inspired Scripture imposed upon us. The close interrelationship of Scripture and community, on the other hand, means that the inspiration of the biblical materials began already with the first formulation of those traditions and continued as they were reshaped and reformulated during their transmission within the ongoing community. Rather than being inspired only at the final stage of transmission, when they were written down in the biblical books we now have, those traditions, shaped by the community which existed for God's purposes and by his providence, shared in divine inspiration from their inception. Inspiration is therefore to be located as much in the community of faith, out of whose experience traditions were formulated and reformulated, as in the process of giving final shape to the biblical books.

Such an understanding of inspiration resolves the intractable problems associated with the understanding of the inspiration of Scripture in terms of the prophetic model, i.e., one person writing one inspired Scripture. To be sure, such individual composition of literature is still to be understood within the overall concept of inspiration.

It is to be understood, however, as part of that process in the community which sought to express its faith by means of traditions that were formulated and reformulated, both to give them more accurate expression and to adapt them to new and changing situations. Thus, the composition of Scripture is not so much the point of inspiration as it is the culmination of the process by means of which the community sought to express its understanding of its own history with God.

That may also, incidentally, explain why the overwhelming majority of authors, i.e., those who gave the present form to the books in our Bible, remain anonymous. If the composition of Scripture is so closely tied to the life of the community out of which it grows, then the final composition cannot be understood as the point at which inspiration occurs. Indeed, it is not even the point at which composition of the material may be located, since much of the material came in the form of traditions that had already received their "composition." The anonymity of Scripture may thus be intimately tied to the fact that Scripture's origin lies far more within the community than in an individual, and may indeed bear witness that inspiration is to be understood in a broader sense than simply as an inspired individual producing an inspired book.[15]

To understand the origin of inspired Scripture in such a way makes clear the glaring fault of understanding Scripture to be an answer book, errorless in all it touches, which an individual can use in isolation in order to learn the "truth." The close relationship of community and Scripture would indicate that such Scripture can only be misunderstood if it is read in isolation from the community of faith which continues to exist as the covenant people and which understands itself in terms of the events that lie at the fountainhead of all

---

[15] The letters of the New Testament constitute the largest exception, although many of them name several persons as responsible for their form, e.g. 1 Cor. 1:1 (Paul and Sosthenes), 1 Thess. 1:1 (Paul, Silas, and Timothy), or Gal. 1:1–2 (Paul and all the brethren who are with me). In other cases it would appear a number of the letters call upon the authority of the person named as sender rather than actually having been written by that person, e.g., the epistles of Peter and James. As the letter to the Hebrews and the Johannine epistles show, however, even such material can be anonymous. The prophetic books do not constitute an exception, since it is highly unlikely that the prophets themselves are responsible for the present form of the books that bear their respective names.

biblical traditions. If, as Paul affirms, the Spirit is given to the community for its common good (1 Cor. 12, esp. v. 7; cf. also Acts 2:1–4), and if it is the Spirit who gives to Scripture such inspiration as it has, then one cannot dispense with the community and still hope to understand the witness of the Bible. To be sure, individuals may learn much about the faith by reading Scripture, but in the end such a person must become related to the community or such learning can only be understood as distorted. Bible and community belong together, and to ignore the one is to distort the other.[16]

IMPORTANCE OF CANON FORMATION

The third of the key elements to be considered, in addition to the witness of Scripture concerning its own inspiration and the nature of the relationship between community and Scripture, is the way in which the canon of Scriptures was formed. A careful consideration of that process will aid us in our attempts to come to an understanding of the inspiration of the Bible.

The importance of the concept of a "canon," i.e., a normative set of writings, has seldom been understood in its key relationship to the problem of the inspiration of Scripture. It is important simply because the boundaries of inspiration are precisely the boundaries imposed by the canonical limitation. No conservative would want to argue, for example, that when 2 Timothy 3:16 referred to the inspiration of Scripture, that passage referred also to such books as the *Gospel of Thomas* or the *Acts of Paul and Thecla*. Clearly supposed in all arguments about the inspiration of Scripture is the tacit assumption that only those books included in the canon are inspired, and those outside are not. That is, after all, the meaning of *canon*. Yet what that really means is that the canon is a key element in understanding the inspiration of Scripture, since it delimits the area within which inspiration is understood to have operated. God inspired the canonical books, with no

---

[16] On the communal aspect of inspiration, see Rahner's book *Inspiration in the Bible*, MacKenzie's article "The Social Character of Inspiration," and Vawter, *Biblical Inspiration*, 158–59. I have learned much from all three. On the problem in this context with Biblicism, see John H. Leith, *Assembly at Westminster: Reformed Theology in the Making* (Richmond: John Knox Press, 1973), 80–81.

exception, and no noncanonical books are inspired, with no exception. The key to the inspiration of Scripture is therefore the existence of the canon. It is the canon, after all, that tells us which Scriptures are inspired and which are not.[17]

When we come to investigate how those canonical limits were determined, however, we begin to glimpse the difficulties it poses for understanding the inspiration of Scripture in terms of the prophetic model, simply because there is no similar model for determining canonical limits. It has often been affirmed that just as the New Testament was based on apostolic testimony, so was the boundary of the canon.[18] Yet if that were the case, how could it have happened that it took so very long, with so much disputation, to agree on the boundaries of the canon? A glance at the history of the canonical process makes clear that there was, from the beginning, lack of agreement on which books belong in the canon, as there was on what the criteria for inclusion ought to be. Some books were accepted at an early time, later rejected, and still later included (e.g., the Revelation of John). Other books were accepted very late (e.g., the Epistle of James), while still others were accepted fairly early on, only to be rejected later (e.g., the *Epistle of Barnabas*). If the boundaries of the canon are apostolically determined, why was there so little agreement on what that apostolic determination was? In fact, however, the boundaries of the canon were simply not determined in accordance with any apostolic pronouncement or decree. The canon was assembled over a long period of time, with opinions differing in different parts of the church, and indeed with opinions differing in the same areas at different periods of time. The canon, in short, was only finally determined on the basis of long experience of the church with a large variety of writings, some of which, in that collective experience, were to be included in the canon, and hence to be regarded as authoritatively inspired, while others were to be excluded, and hence to be regarded as lacking in such inspiration.

---

[17] One can of course argue that other books are "inspired"; even the church fathers attributed some of the things they said to the Spirit of God at work within them. Yet none of those writings achieved the authoritative status accorded to the writings included in the canon. It is in that authoritative sense that we are using the word *inspiration* in this discussion.

[18] For a discussion of this point, see Rahner, *Inspiration in the Bible,* 64–65.

If there are problems with the canonical boundaries being apostolic, however, there are also problems with the actual event of "closing" the canon. While the synods of Hippo (A.D. 393) and Carthage (A.D. 397) are often cited as the point at which the canon was finally and officially closed,[19] that decision was not accepted, for example, by the Syrian churches. They apparently did not agree to the present canon until sometime in the late sixth or early seventh century. The additional problem for Protestants, however, lies in the fact that the synods of Hippo and Carthage included in the canonical lists the books that Protestants call the Apocrypha. No conservative Protestant, one suspects, would want to accord to the book of Tobit or 1 Maccabees the same status of inspired Scripture accorded to the book of Genesis or the Gospel of John. For that matter, one doubts that many contemporary Protestants of any persuasion would be likely to regard the apocryphal books as belonging in the canon on a par with the other sixty-six books. The decision to exclude the Apocrypha was made at the time of the Reformation. That means that reflection on the boundaries of the canon continued some fourteen centuries or more after the last canonical book is likely to have been written.

All of this renders it doubtful in the extreme that when the composers of 2 Timothy and 2 Peter made statements about Scripture, they had in mind only those writings which were finally determined to belong to the group of inspired Scripture in the sixteenth century! If we want to continue to affirm that canonical biblical books are inspired in a way no other human writings are, we are going to have to revise our concept of inspiration as an inspired author producing an inspired piece of literature. There is simply no comparable model for understanding the inspiration of the canonical limits. Yet if the canonical limits are correct, and include only inspired literature and exclude only uninspired literature, then those canonical limits will somehow have to share in that same kind of inspiration.

There is another point the formation of the canon can teach us about the way inspiration occurs. It is evident, for example, that many

---

[19] As John Goldingay (*Models for Scripture* [Grand Rapids: Eerdmans, 1994], 105) points out, we know of no point at which either Jewish or Christian canon was definitively closed; we have rather de facto acknowledgment of canonical limits, as in Athanasius's Thirty-Ninth Festal Letter (A.D. 367) or in the Council of Hippo (A.D. 393). See Migne, *PL* lvi, cols. 428–429). See also e.g., Berkouwer, *Holy Scripture,* 70.

of the books contained in the canon are compilations of materials that exist in several places in often identical form within the canon. For example, Psalm 14 is repeated as Psalm 53;[20] Psalm 18 is repeated in 2 Samuel 22; Psalm 70 is included in Psalm 40 (vs. 13–17); Psalm 57:7–11 is the same as Psalm 108:1–5; with a small exception (Isa. 38:9–20), Isaiah 36 to 39 is similar to 2 Kings 18:13 to 20:19; and much of Jude 4–16 is repeated in 2 Peter 2:1–18.[21] Clearly, as the individual psalms that we have in our canon were put into small, and then into larger collections, favorite materials from smaller collections simply were also included in the larger collections. In short, the book of Psalms was assembled by much the same process as the canon itself: over long periods, certain materials proved themselves in the experience of the faithful community to be useful, and were included in the sacred literature.[22]

A final observation about the formation of the canon is useful: the canon was formed, or at least the process of canonical formation was hastened, and the form of the New Testament canon was significantly shaped, in response to the attempt by Marcion to form his own canon in the second century of our era. Marcion sought to limit the Christian witness essentially to the theological insights of the apostle Paul, and sought further to emphasize Paul's negative judgments on the law of the Old Testament. As a result, Marcion's canon consisted of letters of Paul, with favorable references to the law excised, and a gospel, apparently a form of the Gospel of Luke that had been similarly edited. While the basic format of "gospel and apostle" may have thus been given the church by Marcion, who was later rejected as a heretic, the church responded by expanding the number of gospels and of apostles (by including letters by other "apostles") to form our present canon. Further difficulties with the Gnostics, and with Montanus, who

---

[20] Psalm 14 identifies God as "Yahweh," Ps. 53 as "Elohim," indicating that the same psalm was used in different parts of Israel and adapted to the preferred religious terminology.

[21] I owe the Old Testament examples to Beegle, *Scripture, Tradition, and Infallibility,* 243–44. The chapter "Plenary Inspiration and the Canon" is well worth reading.

[22] Theologically speaking, the church did not create the canon so much as it came to recognize it, as Goldingay (*Models for Scripture,* 177) asserts. Similarly, the church did not bestow authority on the canonical writings so much as it recognized the authority already there, as Gnuse (*Authority of the Bible,* 110) observes.

claimed that the Holy Spirit spoke through him as it had through the original disciples, made it evident that some norm for faith had to be established. In that way the canonical process was given added urgency. Perhaps the church would eventually have formed a canon without the impulse of those internal struggles, but in fact the canon we now have bears the marks of the church's response to those challenges.

The canon, therefore, was formed in much the same way as was much of the prophetic literature and many of the letters of Paul: namely, as responses to new situations that represented threats to the life of the community of faith. What all of this means, in summary, is that the formation of the Christian canon as the boundary by means of which the church is to distinguish between inspired and noninspired Scripture proceeded in a way that makes it impossible to apply to its formation the model normally applied to the production of the individual pieces of Scripture, namely, the prophetic model of one person writing one book. The historical procedure that was followed in selecting the canon, a procedure that for Protestants continued over a span of some fifteen hundred years, simply cannot be reduced to the prophetic model. Rather, the canon emerged as the result of community reflections on the common traditions in the light of the changing historical situation. It is that model, rather than the prophetic one, which we want to urge as more appropriate for understanding the process by which inspired Scripture was produced.

We have concluded our examination of three key components necessary for understanding the nature of Scripture and its inspiration: namely, the witness of Scripture itself to its inspiration and nature, the relationship between community and Scripture, and the formation of the Christian canon. Bearing in mind the insights we have gained from these examinations, we must turn now to a consideration of the way the inspiration of Scripture is to be understood, given the realities we have uncovered about the actual nature of the Bible. Our task is to discover a view of inspiration of Scripture which is consonant with the nature of Scripture, rather than conceiving inspiration in terms of some prior category imposed upon Scripture from the outside, i.e., factual inerrancy. We must also find a way other than the prophetic model, whose inadequacies we have now seen. We shall suggest instead that the interaction of three key components must be understood if we are to arrive at a clear conception of the way in which inspiration has been at work in the composition of the books of our Bible: the traditions of the faithful community, the situation facing that community, and the compiler of those traditions into a piece of literature, i.e., the "author." While we shall urge that inspiration occurs in the convergence of these three components, we need, for the sake of clarity, to examine each one separately before we consider how they interact. We shall turn our attention first to an examination of the "traditions."

THREE KEY COMPONENTS

Traditions

In our earlier discussion of traditions in relation to the way contemporary critical scholarship views the nature of biblical literature, we saw that traditions are the means by which the community understands itself in relation to its past. Key events in the past become the substance of the traditions by means of which the community understands itself and shapes its life in accordance with that past. Traditions guard those past events which give to the community its uniqueness, and they aid the community in shaping its life in accordance with those originating events. Thus, the event of the exodus and reflections on its significance gave shape and a central focus as well as a continuing impetus to much of the traditional material contained in the Old Testament. Similarly, the event of Jesus Christ, especially his death and resurrection, and reflection on the meaning of those events, gave structure to the traditions formulated by the early church. Continuing reflection on those constitutive events and the traditions they set in motion, represented in the biblical literature, sought to keep the community true to those foundational events which gave to the community its uniqueness. scriptural traditions therefore are intended to keep the community's life and faith in conformity with the nature and implications of the community's foundational, and hence constitutive, events.[23]

The origin of a tradition is furthermore an event that engenders a hope strong enough to affect the life of a community, a hope that

---

[23] Because of such normative intentions, scriptural traditions contain within themselves the suppositions necessary to form a *canon*, i.e., something against which something else is measured.

finds expression in the traditions themselves, and that is continually renewed in contact with those traditions.[24] The exodus thus engendered the hope that the band of escaping slaves would one day possess a land and live in accordance with God's will for his chosen people. The Old Testament literature shows how that hope achieved concrete reality and also how that reality was judged and evaluated in terms of the original event that inspired the primal hope. The Christ event similarly engendered the hope that the Kingdom of God which Jesus announced would in fact become reality, a hope given final impetus by his resurrection. The letters of Paul, to be sure, but even the Gospels themselves, show how that primal hope produced traditions by which the community sought to shape its life, and how the traditions appealed to that primal hope in measuring and correcting the structure and activity of the community.

Biblical traditions therefore remember the past for the sake of the present and the future. While in such a situation the past is, to be sure, of great importance, it is not of conclusive importance. What is important is the way that past is able to function, indeed how it ought to function, to shape the present in accordance with the reality to which the tradition points. Traditions are therefore not primarily concerned with historical fact so much as they are concerned with the significance of those past events for the present, and the promise they hold for the future. It is for that reason that such traditions can err in factual matters, statistics and the like, without in any way compromising their truth as *traditions*. Given the nature of tradition, it is sheer perversity to want to find statistical accuracy in them, and to want to judge their value and validity by the presence or absence of such elements. In such matters, the traditions are dependent on ordinary channels of information, and are heir to all the problems inherent in the verbal transmission of factual information. What makes those traditions inspired is not any such statistical accuracy, but their witness to the ongoing presence of God with a community that looks to a decisive act of that God as its constitutive origin. The extent to which traditions carry out their task of representing to the community the

---

[24] The fact that hope is a constitutive element of the engendering event and the ensuing foundation traditions is anchored in the reality of the God who brings about the engendering event. That God is a God not limited to the past, but is the One in whose hands the future also lies.

activity it must pursue and the shape it must assume in the light of the originating act of God is the extent to which they are inspired. It is the witness of that tradition that, apart from the continuing presence of that God, no such faithful shaping of community life would be possible. Apart from the continuing presence and guidance of the Spirit, no activity consonant with the founding event could occur. In fact, the continuing presence of that Spirit finds the vehicle for that presence precisely in the traditions that remind the community of the origin it had, and hence of the goal it is to pursue. It is that use by the Spirit of God which makes those traditions inspired.

Such traditions, therefore, represent the concretion of the ways in which the community has sought to structure itself in accordance with its originating event, and which, in turn, provide the framework in which new generations understand themselves and their task. Traditions provide the cradle in which each new generation of the community is nurtured. They provide contact with the past event that shapes their present and gives them hope for their future, and therefore traditions represent the historical reality of the community. To be out of touch with those traditions is to be out of touch with the reality upon which the community depends for its unique existence. The traditions are the building materials out of which the community continues to construct itself and to shape its present and its future.

We have also seen, however, that those traditions represent not so much a static element, although they do act to conserve the past, as a dynamic element, which continually calls for a faithful response to that past in the light of the changing situation of the present. What gives to tradition this dynamic nature is the second of the three elements in the convergence of which we may discern the inspiration of Scripture. That second element we may call the "situation" to which the traditions must respond.

Situation

If, as we have seen, traditions take their origin as the response to an event of primal importance for the community of faith, it is also true that those traditions are used, and modified, when that same community faces new situations. If the traditions are the framework within which the community understands itself, its past, and on that

basis its future, they are also the means whereby the community seeks
to understand new situations into which it is thrust by its existence in
the historical arena. It is precisely when those traditions are used to
understand the new situation that the modification of tradition occurs
which is so much a characteristic of the biblical literature. When a
nomadic Hebrew people moves in from the desert to take possession
of Canaan, an agricultural land, the traditions of the desert must be
reinterpreted in order to allow the community of nomads to remain
faithful to its origins within the radically changed situation in which
the nomads then find themselves. Evidences of that are clear in the
collections of laws in the Pentateuch, and in the stories of the books of
Joshua and Judges, as the nomadic tribes seek to find, within the
structure of their old traditions, a new mode of organizing themselves
while yet remaining the people God summoned out of Egypt and to
whom he gave a promised land. The dual tradition of kingship in 1 and
2 Samuel in which the idea of kingship is seen now as a blessing from
God, now as a curse on an unfaithful people, shows the struggle such
new situations imposed on the older traditions as the community
sought to use them to understand its new situation.

When Israel had become a nation among other nations, and was
hence caught up in the political machinations of its time, the traditions that had allowed Israel to understand its emergence as a nation,
i.e., the promise of a land for themselves and their heirs, became not
so much a vehicle for adapting the people to God's will as an excuse to
cease facing ever new situations into which they were thrust. Threat-
ened with becoming simply another geopolitical entity in the world
of its time, Israel was reminded by its prophets that the chosen people
may not become just another political entity. The fundamental reinterpretation of the meaning of Israel's existence which the prophets
carried out was nevertheless done in terms of the old traditions, the
covenants on Sinai and with David, the promise of land and descendants
to Abraham, the traditions of the time of desert wanderings. The
prophets drew on all of them, but transformed them in the light of
the current situation in new ways in which both past and future, and
thus present, were to be understood. The prophets warn a people
grown complacent on the basis of election and promised land that the
God who gave the land can also take it away, and summon that
community grown listless in the faith to realize that they depend

solely on God's decision to allow them to remain a people. The very traditions on which they depended and from which they gained confidence in their nationhood were the ones used by the prophets to announce exile and an end to such nationhood.

To a shattered people in exile, occupied with remembering the past and seeking to justify it despite the negative judgment of the present upon it, new prophets arose and announced a restoration. Using the very traditions of a God who created and then destroyed a nation, these prophets announced God's new creative act on his people's behalf. Again, ancient traditions were used and recast in an attempt to understand the new situation now confronting God's chosen people. Attempts to create a theocracy along priestly lines, to establish an independent political entity through open rebellion, to preserve identity through centralized rituals—all were tried, and all called upon the ancient traditions to understand and justify the new situation. When finally a figure arose who announced, again on the basis of those ancient yet living traditions, that the restoration was to be in yet another form, those traditions underwent one more transformation. Understanding himself within the framework of the Israel whose descendant he was, Jesus announced his message, as had the prophets, historians, revolutionaries, and lawyers before him, in terms of the God of Israel and the traditions to which his acts had given rise. His followers did the same, and the letters of Paul contain those reinterpreted traditions of the past, recast now to meet the new situation, one in which the long-promised messiah had come.

In all such instances, new situations forced reexamination and recasting of tradition, providing the community of faith with a dynamic and living traditional base upon which to build and in terms of which to understand its past in the light of its changing present and future. In each instance, the reinterpreted traditions became the framework on which the next generation sought to understand itself in the light of the new situation it faced. The reinterpreted traditions by which Israel defined its nationhood became the basis for yet another prophetic reinterpretation, just as subsequently the prophetic reinterpretation became the basis for the further recasting of those traditions within the Christian community. That same process can be observed at work within the Christian literature as well. Each Gospel makes use of the Jesus traditions to meet the particular problems faced by the community for which it is written, a process that becomes clear when one compares how the same accounts from the life of Jesus are presented in the various Gospels. Paul does the same in his correspondence as he seeks to make clear on the basis of both Old Testament and Christian traditions what it means to live in the new age, in a community which knows that the ancient promise of a deliverer has now been fulfilled.

It is also clear, as we saw earlier, that when the Old Testament is used, in quotation and paraphrase, in the New Testament writings, it is being used in precisely the same way that traditions from the past are regularly used to illumine the contemporary situation. Just as prophets were willing to find a new meaning in older traditions in order to illuminate the significance of the new situation to which they felt compelled to respond; just as Jesus was willing to find a new meaning in older legal traditions in order to illuminate the significance of the new situation brought about by his presence—so the creators and transmitters of New Testament traditions were willing to find in certain portions of the Old Testament new meanings to illuminate the new situation created by the resurrection of Jesus and the Spirit-empowered creation of the new community of faith. If, in order to make clear that new significance, words were changed or emphases relocated, it simply means that in that manner those old traditions were being shaped to bear the new meaning. Seen in this light, the fact that New Testament traditions do not always quote Old Testament material with the precision that historians would like to find means simply that the material was not being quoted with historical intention. Faithful to the way in which traditions had normally, over centuries, been adapted by faithful respondents in new situations, the shapers of the New Testament traditions continued to find in those Old Testament traditions, not archives of historical interest, but living traditions which could be shaped to speak God's new word to the new times. What is at issue is therefore not an attitude toward Scripture, inerrant or otherwise, in the New Testament's use of the Old, but rather the unbroken continuation of the prophetic use in new situations of older traditions, reshaped to bear the truth of new situations.

In this long process covered by our biblical literature, as new situations arise they are understood in the framework of traditions that grew out of past situations, but these in turn are then reinterpreted for the present. That reinterpretation in its turn becomes the traditions upon which the next generation seeks to understand itself, and which, in the light of its changing situation, must once more find a new interpretation. Hence, although the past informs and thus shapes the future, the past is also open to the dynamic process of growth and interpretative change. As a result, each successive new generation has an enlarged traditional base from which to draw its own understanding of itself and its new situation. In that way, through the pressure of the situation, traditions assume a dynamic form and become the justification for change as they do for preservation of past values. Our Scriptures contain the repetitions, tensions, discrepancies, and differing interpretations that they do precisely because they contain within themselves the whole variety of interpretations and reinterpretations that the living community of faith has undertaken as it sought to understand its past and to respond faithfully to its present. The sedimentation of a living tradition, which grew and changed with changing situations, our Bible is not an archive of dead, treasured memories of the past, but the record of living traditions which because of their origins continue to provide guidance, and the basis for ever-new interpretations for the community of faith right to the present day. It is the ever-changing response of tradition to new situation that has given to our sacred Scriptures the characteristics they display and which must be taken into account in any attempt to understand how they have been inspired.[25]

In the understanding of that Scripture itself, the new situations into which the community of faith emerged, both in the Old and New Testaments, were not the result of blind historical forces, nor were the responses haphazard. The community of faith, appearances to the contrary notwithstanding, is never totally removed from the guidance of God or the presence of his Spirit. For that reason, new situations and the new interpretations of tradition they elicited are understood by Scripture to be further evidence of the care and providence of the living God. If Israel and the church find the presence of God's Spirit in the primal event of their existence, and in the traditions that event summoned forth, they also find that presence in the new situations

---

[25] Excellent discussions of the dynamic vitality of Old Testament traditions and the process by which they were assembled into the books as we have them can be found in Brueggemann and Wolff, *The Vitality of Old Testament Traditions,* and in Sanders, *Torah and Canon.*

confronting them, and seek to follow the guidance of that same Spirit in their reinterpretations of their traditions. It is for that reason that the dynamic nature of the traditions contained in our biblical writings points to their inspiration and must be acknowledged as playing a key role in any attempt to understand the inspiration of Scripture. It is that very dynamic nature that points to the continuing guidance of God's Spirit in the times our Scripture was being formed.

Respondent

We have now examined two of the three components in whose convergence we are to understand the inspiration of Scripture, namely, tradition and situation. Yet left to themselves, these two components would remain mute, indeed would never come into existence as a result of the primal event and the changing situation. A third component is necessary if tradition is to arise and be reinterpreted in the new situations. That component is the respondent, understood broadly as anyone who contributes to the formulation and reformulation of tradition in specific situations.[26]

Obviously, without that kind of respondent, traditions would never begin, to say nothing of being reinterpreted in a new situation. Without a prophet, the new application of tradition to the current situation would simply not occur. Without a historian, traditions would not experience reevaluation in the light of changing historical circumstances. Without an evangelist, the traditions about Jesus would never be organized in coherent form to meet the needs of some community of faith. To that extent, the respondent is identical to the "author" of Scripture.

Yet we want to understand respondent in a far broader way than simply as the person who has accorded to any given book in the Bible its final form. If that person alone be an author, and hence in some way a participant in inspiration, who has written the book in the form we

---

[26] In defense of propositional theology, some conservatives like to point out that unless God were to speak, the events he occasions would remain mute. It is precisely the need of someone to speak, and to say here God is active, and here God is not, normally assigned to the prophetic voice, that is represented in what I am terming the "respondent." It is the respondent who, motivated by the Spirit of the God who occasions the events, tells us where God is active in the present and responds to that activity in the language of the community's traditions.

now have it, then the prophet whose words another has recorded in their present form would not be part of the inspiration of Scripture. Amos would not be the inspired person in regard to the book bearing his name, but rather the inspired person would be the nameless assembler who collected the materials, edited them, and put them in their present order with a short appendix. We want to affirm, on the other hand, that not only that final compiler but also Amos himself, as a respondent to a new situation who reinterprets tradition, plays a significant role in the inspiration of the Scripture we have. Not only the nameless person or persons who assembled our Pentateuch belong to the act of scriptural inspiration but also the equally nameless people who formulated, retold, and adapted the traditions that went into the sources which were used by the compilers of the books that were assembled into the Pentateuch belong to that divinely guided process by which inspired Scripture was produced. Not only the evangelist who gave the Gospel of Mark its final form can be thought of as respondent but those who first formulated the traditions about Jesus, who used and adapted them in their proclamation of the event of Christ, as well as those who began to assemble collections of similar stories, belong among the respondents who interpreted traditions in their situation and who have thus produced the inspired Scripture that we have.

Understood in that way, the respondents may remain nameless so long as we have the results of their labors. It is really not important that the apostle Paul may not have written 1 Timothy, since that book, like many others in Scripture, may have behind it a series of respondents, one of whom at an earlier stage may have been Paul, whose own traditions have since been modified in new situations by further respondents. Understood in that way, we can also allow the proper role to the community of faith which played so large a part in the preservation and interpretation of traditions in new situations. As the recipients and preservers of reinterpreted traditions, they, too, played their role as respondents in the creation of our inspired Scriptures. To be sure, communities as such do not write books, individuals do. But to put the total weight of inspiration on that final individual who sets down the results of a long process of formulation and reformulation, as is the case when one understands inspiration on the prophetic model, is to make a mockery of the intimate relationship between Scripture and community and to deny to key individuals—Jesus, the prophets, apostles—their true role in the production of inspired Scripture. It is not only the final assembler or compiler or author who shares in the inspiration which has produced Scripture. Rather, inspiration must be understood to be at work in all who have shaped, preserved, and assembled portions of the traditions contained in the several books.[27]

The impossible task of finding some apostle as author of every New Testament book, so that it may be regarded as inspired, is thus shown to be unnecessary at the outset. Similarly, the problem of an errorless autograph that alone is worthy to bear the weight of inspiration is seen to be an exercise in futility, as though at only one point, and in only one formulation, the traditions assembled in a given book of Scripture could be called inspired. Rather, inspiration is at work down the whole process as respondent after respondent carried on the task of preserving and adapting traditions upon which alone the life of the community of faith can responsibly be formed. Unless the Spirit be present with each respondent who helped shape the traditions from which our Scriptures were formed, it is difficult to see how a collection of those traditions could be understood to be inspired, however much the Spirit may have been present with that compiler. Rather, the final compiler is to be understood as one more respondent who, faithful to the promptings of God's Spirit, has responded to the new situation by reinterpreting the traditions through the act of assembling them into a larger work.

THE LOCUS OF INSPIRATION

It is therefore in the interrelationship of the three components of Scripture—tradition, situation, and respondent—that the inspiration of Scripture is to be located. Inspiration thus describes more the process out of which our Scriptures grew than simply the final result in canonical form.[28] This of course is not to disparage in any way that

---

[27] This idea was given cogent expression by Orr, *Revelation and Inspiration,* esp. 194–95.

[28] In discussing true and false prophecy, James Sanders, in his essay in Coats and Long, eds., *Canon and Authority,* identifies three components: hermeneutics, text/traditions, and context/situations. Although I had formulated the three components discussed in this chapter before I read Professor Sanders's article, and though he uses his triad to resolve somewhat different problems, I happily recognize the similarity of our thinking about the biblical text.

canonical form. It is the only form we have of sacred Scripture, and is surely to be understood as coming into being in accordance with the will of God, i.e., as inspired. It is to say, however, that we cannot, on the model of the prophetic understanding of inspiration, assume that such inspiration occurred only at the point that some author set down the canonical form we have. Rather, the final form is the culmination of a process of the growth of Scripture that began with the primal event that shaped the community of faith and that has continued through the process of forming and reforming the tradition on the part of faithful respondents to new situations confronting that community.[29]

A comparison with the formation of the canon is appropriate at this point. As we saw, no one person made a final decision on the closing of the canon. In fact, no formal decision was ever made, at least so far as Protestants are concerned. Various confessions contain references to the scope of the canon, but no formal conclave ever decided canonical boundaries. Rather, the experience of the church as the community of faith has determined which books are useful for the life of that community and which are less useful. Canonical limits come at the end, not at the beginning, of a long process. Similarly, Scripture has grown out of the experience of the church as the community of faith, with various traditions which are recognized as primal for the existence of that community and which are shaped and reshaped as the situation confronting the believing community changes. It is probably as difficult, and as pointless, to seek the individuals who gave to each of the various books of the Bible its final shape, as it is to find the point at which the canon was "closed." The respondent who gave to a

---

[29] A number of authors have now located inspiration in the process rather than the text; e.g., John M. Lewis, *Revelation, Inspiration, Scripture* (*Layman's Library of Christian Doctrine,* vol. 3 [Nashville: Broadman, 1985]), 50: God was involved in the writing, editing, collection and preservation of the written witness to revealing redemptive acts; I. Howard Marshall, *Biblical Inspiration* (Grand Rapids: Eerdmans, 1982), 42: the Spirit was active in the whole procedure of oral and literary processes underlying Scripture; Abraham, *Divine Inspiration,* 67: God inspires through his personal guidance of those who wrote and put together the various parts of the Bible. Even Bloesch (*Holy Scripture,* 119–20), who still wants to speak of the inspiration of the "prophet," redefines prophet in such a way as to involve the entire process of biblical composition: "By the biblical prophets I have in mind all preachers, writers and editors in biblical history . . . " (120).

particular book its final form was heir to a history of the community of faith which had provided that respondent with the traditions which had stood the test of time and which the community deemed useful to preserve. For that reason, inspiration must be seen in the long process by which the content, not only the final form, of the various biblical books was produced.[30]

That also means, given the plethora of traditions produced and interpreted in the life of the community of faith, both Israel and the church, that the inspired nature of certain of those traditions is an a posteriori discovery, not an a priori assumption. Just as the canon resulted only after centuries of experience with a variety of Christian writings that determined some to be more valuable than others, so the traditions that comprise the various books, the situations that called them forth, and the respondents who shaped them at the various stages were evaluated in the experience of the community of faith. In that experience, some traditions were found to be of more value and were included in the ongoing traditions of the community. In that way, the responses of some to new situations on the basis of tradition came to be regarded as false, and such "false prophets," for example, were then discredited. That was not an instant decision, however. Rarely, if ever, was the true prophet accorded instant recognition while the false prophet was summarily rejected. Far more often, the reverse was true. Only after the community evaluated the various responses, sometimes over decades or even centuries, did the truth of the various respondents become clear. If time was required to determine which were the canonical books, time was also required to determine which were the appropriate responses in the tradition to various situations, and the inspiration of the Holy Spirit must be understood to have been at work within the entire process rather than merely at a single point. It was, as we have suggested, from the interrelationship of tradition, situation, and respondent that the Holy Spirit summoned forth the words of Scripture. It is in such a dynamic way that inspiration is best understood, and, we would urge,

---

[30] James Orr is the earliest author of whom I am aware who assigned inspiration to the process by which Scripture was produced, rather than simply to the moment when the canonical form was achieved; see his *Revelation and Inspiration*, esp. ch. 9.

that best allows us to account for the way in which Scripture was in fact produced.

Such an understanding of inspiration has a number of implications, such as the relationship of the Holy Spirit to the past and present community of faith, the relationship of preaching to the inspiration of Scripture, and the way Scripture is intended to be used within the community of faith, i.e., its authority. We shall devote the final pages of this book to a brief exploration of some of those implications.

Chapter 6

Some Implications

Our investigation into the nature of the biblical writings and the way we are to understand their inspiration has led us to urge that such inspiration is to be found in the confluence of the three components of Scripture: tradition, situation, and respondent. We have urged that inspiration must be understood in the dynamic process of that confluence rather than in some static sense of identifying one author as the inspired source of one inspired piece of writing. That way of understanding inspiration simply does not fit the way Scripture came into existence. It is the continuing presence of the Spirit in the continual coming together of those three components which allows us to affirm that the Bible is "inspired," that is, that uniquely among books, it points beyond itself to the God who created, sustains, and will save his creation. There is a further work of the Spirit which must be discussed in our consideration of the inspiration of Scripture, however. That work is classically defined as the internal testimony of the Holy Spirit (*testimonium internum Spiritus Sancti*).

INTERNAL TESTIMONY OF THE HOLY SPIRIT

It is clear enough that however we may want to affirm the inspiration of our written Scripture, the reading or hearing of it does not necessarily lead to understanding it or to accepting its witness as true. What to Paul was sober truth was to Festus sheer madness (Acts 26:24–25). Though the Sadducees revere the Torah, Jesus tells them they do not know the Scripture they themselves have read (Mark 12:24, 26). Indeed, it is the fate of many to see but not perceive, to hear but not understand (4:12). Some further act is necessary before the words of Scripture are able to convince the reader or hearer of their truth. It is that further act which is described as the inner testimony of the Holy Spirit.[1] On this doctrine, it is not the indicia of the Scriptures that convince us of their truth, nor the majesty of their prose, nor the grandeur of the subject matter, nor even the historic veneration in which the church has held it. Without the internal testimony of the Spirit, Scripture remains mute in its witness to the truth.[2]

That insight is of central importance for any understanding of the inspiration of Scripture because it is clear evidence that that inspiration does not in fact cease with the production of the writing but must also continue with the reading, or "inspiration" does not describe a significant reality. That is of course not to say that the Scriptures contain no truth unless someone recognizes it. The true witness is there, recognized or not. Yet it will not function as witness until the recognition takes place. It is just the insight into the necessity of this internal testimony of the Spirit, therefore, which confirms our insight that we must understand inspiration in terms of a process rather than in a more static way as limited to the individual authorship of individual books. Not only the nature of Scripture itself, comprised of traditions, situation, and respondent, points to the need to understand inspiration within the total process of the community of the faithful seeking to respond in a responsible way to God's revelation, but the further insight that until that same Spirit who inspired the process of the creation of Scripture also inspires its use, no witness occurs, points to the correctness of our analysis of the way inspiration occurs. Unless inspiration continues to the reading and hearing of Scripture, Scripture remains a museum piece, of interest to antiquarians who want to

---

[1] On this topic, see Berkouwer, *Holy Scripture*, ch. 2, "The Testimony of the Spirit," esp. 55–57; John Calvin, *Institutes*, I. vii. 4; Heppe, *Die Theologie der evangelisch-reformierten Kirche*, ch. 1, *"De Scriptura Sacra."*

[2] This point is made explicitly in the Westminster Confession, 1, 5; see also Calvin, *Institutes*, I. vii. 5; Luther: "Where (the Holy Spirit) openeth not Scripture, it is not understood" (quoted in D. Bloesch, "The Primacy of Scripture," in D. McKim, ed., *The Authoritative Word: Essays on the Nature of Scripture* [Grand Rapids: Eerdmans, 1983], 120); Orr, *Revelation and Inspiration*, ch. 10, sec. I; D. Bloesch, *Holy Scripture: Revelation, Inspiration, and Interpretation* (*Christian Foundations*, Downers Grove, Ill.: InterVarsity Press, 1994), 89, 114.

affirm that at one time the Spirit of God inspired a collection of writings, whose present utility is no greater than that of any other object from the remote past. The continuing existence of the community of faith shows that in fact the Spirit has continued to inspire the reading of Scripture, and hence inspiration must be understood as a continuing process, not one that ended when the last word of the last biblical book was penned.

A second point needs to be observed in relation to the internal testimony of the Spirit and the inspiration of Scripture. That point is simply the fact that in the classic understanding of the internal testimony, it is always related, not to Scripture as a phenomenon, but to the *content* of Scripture. That is, the inward testimony convinces the reader of the truth of the content of what he or she reads, rather than anything about the external nature of the witness, i.e., the actual books themselves. Scripture is never the object of the Spirit's testimony apart from its content. That means simply that while the inner testimony can convince me that what the Bible says is true, it does not convince me in any way about how the witness was assembled (e.g., on a prophetic model where an inspired individual wrote an inspired book), or about how the witness is to be regarded (e.g., as inerrant in all statements). In sum, one cannot detach the internal testimony of the Holy Spirit from the content of Scripture and appeal to it in defense of the argument that inspired Scripture is by nature inerrant in all statements. The Spirit does not supply any prior certainty regarding the nature of Scripture, from which we may then logically deduce that its content is true. Rather, the Spirit witnesses to the truth of the content of Scripture, and in that way convinces us of its inspired nature.[3]

That has the further implication that the internal testimony of the Spirit is not limited to the written words of Scripture, an implication whose truth is based on the fact that the Holy Spirit is not identical with the written word.[4] Because inspiration begins before the writing of Scripture, and because people have also been convinced of the truth of the content of Scripture from oral as well as from the written form,

---

[3] On this point, see the discussion in Berkouwer, *Holy Scripture,* 41–45; H. Cunliffe-Jones, *The Authority of the Biblical Revelation* (Boston: Pilgrim Press, 1948), 122.

[4] Reid, *Authority of Scripture,* 49–50, has a good discussion of Calvin's view on this point; cf. also Rogers, ed., *Biblical Authority,* 56.

Calvin argued, for example, that one cannot limit inspiration to the written word of Scripture. Instead, the Spirit retains the function of inspiration and does not delegate it to the words of Scripture, but rather uses those words to convince people of the truth of the *content* of the message to which Scripture also bears witness.[5]

Finally, because it is the Spirit who both inspired the Scripture and inspires the readers and hearers of its message, the witness of the one will confirm the other. Indeed, we do not know of the internal witness of the Spirit except from the Scripture to which it applies.[6] That means that there is no place for appeal to the inner testimony of the Spirit to defend wholly subjective interpretations of Scripture, a practice which happens when the witness of the Spirit is detached from the content of Scripture and raised to independent importance.[7] If the Spirit that bears witness to the reader of Scripture is the same Spirit who was at work in the production of the Scripture, then the witness of the two will correspond and reinforce one another. The internal testimony is therefore not to be equated with any subjective religious experience, of either a pietistic or a rationalistic kind.[8] If the internal testimony of the Spirit bears witness to the *truth* of Scripture in terms of content, it also bears witness to the truth of *Scripture* in terms of what it contains. Realistically, that inner testimony can be appealed to only in reference to the content of the Scripture which, in

---

[5] See Reid, *Authority of Scripture,* 48–49; this was essentially Calvin's view. On this basis, I find I. Howard Marshall's comment (*Biblical Inspiration,* Grand Rapids: Eerdmans, 1982, p. 38) in a reference to the first edition of this book that I "want to relate the work of the Spirit today to an assurance of the truth of the particular contents of the Bible rather than to assurance that the Bible as such is the source of truth" unhelpful. It is not the "inspiredness of the resulting book" that is at issue, as he claims, but the inspiredness of what that book contains!

[6] For a discussion of relevant texts related to this point, see Berkouwer, *Holy Scripture,* 50–51; cf. also Barth, *Conversation with the Bible,* 138–39. The references in John 14:16, 26; 15:26; 16:7 to the Spirit are frequently cited in this discussion as well, as, e.g., in John M. Lewis, *Revelation, Inspiration, Scripture (Layman's Library of Christian Doctrine,* vol. 3, Nashville: Broadman, 1985), 59.

[7] This frequently happens in our day when people want to defend a non-biblical position (e.g., the permissibility of homosexual or lesbian sexual practices) by appealing over the head of Scripture, as it were, to Jesus as "God's Word," as though God's Word in Jesus would contradict God's Word in the inspired witness to Jesus and his meaning!

[8] See Barth, *Conversation with the Bible,* 121, 295.

the experience of the community of faith to which the Spirit has been given (cf. Acts 2; 1 Cor. 12), has demonstrated its viability as vehicle of that Spirit. If the Spirit is not bound to the words of Scripture, it nevertheless witnesses to the same truth as that to which Scripture points, and for that reason both Spirit and Scripture bear witness to the same truth.

All of this points us to the validity of the way we have been urging that the inspiration of Scripture be understood, namely, as the continuing presence of the Spirit with the community of faith as it preserved and renewed its traditions in response to the new situations into which God led it. If that insight is confirmed by the classic understanding of the inner testimony of the Holy Spirit, it has in turn some implications for the way Scripture is to be understood and used by the contemporary community of faith. We must explore some of those.

PROCLAMATION

One of the tasks of the community of the faithful which has long been recognized as intimately related to the nature and purpose of Scripture is proclamation. In addition to the responsibility of reading Scripture, the community understands itself to be called upon to announce the content of Scripture, both to its own members and to those still outside the community. Such a call to proclamation can be legitimated by the nature of Scripture itself, particularly the New Testament. The epistles of Paul are intended to instruct and admonish the Christian communities to which they were written, and they were most likely communicated to those communities orally during the time they were gathered for worship. By their nature, therefore, the epistles intend to proclaim the gospel to those who would read and hear them. Again, because the Gospels are understood to be the result of apostolic proclamation of the event of Jesus Christ, the content of that proclamation in its present written form summons the community of the faithful to continue that proclamation in oral form. To be sure, all such proclamation stands under the rule of the written form of Scripture. When the church formed the canon, it committed itself to the rule of those particular written expressions of its faith. Yet the community has also found that the nourishment of the faithful and its missionary enterprises requires more than simply the reading of

Scripture, whether individually or in groups. Proclamation of the content of the message is also essential.[9] That is, it is necessary to interpret the content of the biblical message for contemporary hearers.

It is at this point that the way in which inspiration of Scripture is understood becomes critical for understanding the task of interpretation and proclamation. If, for example, inspiration is understood to have ceased with the final word of the last biblical book to be written, and if what has been written under such inspiration is totally inerrant in every respect, it is not self-evident that such Scripture needs to be proclaimed. The fact that those who hold such a view of Scripture do engage in proclamation is no evidence of the grounding of that task in their view of Scripture. It may as easily be evidence that they are either incapable or unwilling to follow the logical implications of their position. In fact, if the Scriptures are inerrant because of inspiration, and that inspiration ceased with the last writing of Scripture, then any further elucidation of the message can only result in errant exposition, hardly an advantage over reading the inerrant words of Scripture itself, with no uninspired, errant comments added. How could errant words adequately interpret inerrant Scripture? Unless the process by which Scripture was created is somehow at work in its interpretation and proclamation, it is difficult to see why proclamation is advisable, let alone useful.

It is at this point that the way in which we have been seeking to understand the inspiration of Scripture allows us to draw different conclusions about interpretation and proclamation. If, as we have argued, inspiration is to be found in the conjunction of tradition, situation, and respondent, that conjunction of components is also found in interpretation. That is, the situation out of which Scripture grew is the situation confronted in interpretation. When the interpreter as respondent, in his or her own particular situation, faces the text as the traditions of the faith, the situation from which Scripture was summoned forth is repeated. The interpretation of Scripture thus follows along the same lines as its creation, which means that the interpretation of Scripture belongs to the same process by which it was

---

[9] This conviction is shared by Protestants and Catholics alike. See the *Constitution on Divine Revelation,* esp. pars. 17 and 21; the Augsburg Confession, ch. 5; the Westminster Confession, 21, 5.

created. Such interpretation for a new situation of the traditions of the faith is the same procedure by which Amos reinterpreted the traditions of Israel's election by God, or by which Jesus reinterpreted the law in the Sermon on the Mount, or by which Paul reinterpreted the way the law had been understood by his religious contemporaries. Scripture is not violated when it is treated as an entity capable of further interpretation, a procedure quite in line with its origin and nature. Scripture is violated when its nature is assumed to be static and closed, a condition which would logically imply that no further interpretation is possible or useful. God's word in the biblical traditions continually comes to specific situations, addressed to the community of faith in the midst of its historical existence. It is this very vitality in the nature of Scripture and its inspiration which demands that it be newly interpreted for new historical situations.[10]

It is therefore the very nature of Scripture that demands that it be the source of continuing proclamation. If the conjunction of events from which Scripture grew is similar to the conjunction of events present in interpretation, it is even more evident that the same events are present in the proclamation of the content of the biblical witness. Scripture, as we have urged, is composed of traditions, of a situation needing interpretation from those traditions, and of a respondent to undertake that interpretation for the community of faith. That is of course the identical situation out of which the sermon grows. Faced with the traditions, in this case canonical Scripture, the respondent, in this case the minister or priest, must confront the situation of his community in the light of those traditions. The situation out of which Scripture was composed and in which we are to locate its inspiration is thus the same as the situation of the proclamation of that Scripture. It is for that reason the proclamation is to be understood as one of the fundamental marks of the community of faith. The same Holy Spirit at work in the production of inspired Scripture is also at work, and in the same way, in the production of the proclamation of inspired Scripture.

The close parallel between the manner in which inspired Scripture came into existence and the manner in which it continues to be

---

[10]I am drawing here on insights from Vawter, *Biblical Inspiration,* 94, 155; Brueggemann and Wolff, *The Vitality of Old Testament Traditions,* 124–35; Coats and Long, eds., *Canon and Authority,* 38.

proclaimed is, we would want to urge, not accidental. The inspiring presence of the Spirit, at work as the Scriptures were produced, continues to work as the traditions continue to summon forth respondents in ever-new situations. The sermon is thus the essential continuation of the process begun with the foundational events from which the original traditions took their beginning. Preaching is therefore the oral act which repeats the origin of Scripture. It is for that reason that proclamation is essential to the continuing effectiveness of the witness of inspired Scripture, simply because it participates in the same process by which those Scriptures came into existence. Scripture therefore does not merely tolerate interpretation and proclamation; by its very nature it demands them, in order that the inspiring power of the Spirit may continue to work through the traditions. The necessity of the sermon is therefore not contingent upon but essential to the nature of Scripture and its inspiration. It is in the proclamation to the community of faith that the power by which Scriptures were produced becomes available to those who hear anew its message.

It must also be clearly understood, however, that proclamation is not a substitute for, or an addition to, Scripture. It is also clear that the inspiration of the sermon is subordinate to the inspiration of Scripture. That is the significance of the act of the church in choosing certain writings to be normative, i.e., acknowledging a canon. The traditions in that canon point in an authoritative and unrepeatable way to the foundational events of the community of faith, and community that finds its meaning and future in those events. By forming the canon, therefore, the community confesses itself and its faith to be subordinated to those authoritative interpretations of its founding events.

For that reason, even though the process by which the sermon is produced replicates the process by which Scripture came into existence, the measuring rod and touchstone of the sermon nevertheless necessarily remains Scripture.[11] It is the Scripture that measures and validates the sermon, not the sermon that is the measure of the validity of Scripture. The sermon participates in the power of the

---

[11] Bloesch has put it well: "The new light that breaks forth from God's holy Word (John Robinson, d. 1625) does not contradict or supersede this Word but enables us to understand it in a new way—related to the conflicts and issues of the time in which we live" (*Holy Scripture: Revelation, Inspiration, and Interpretation*, 160).

inspiring Spirit only to the extent that it draws its substance and intention from the inspired Scripture. By forming those Scriptures into its canon, the community of faith acknowledged the authoritative shape of its foundational traditions. We are called upon not to lay again that foundation, but to build upon it in our sermons and in our interpretation. To put it another way, in acknowledging its canon, the community of faith declared that its further experience was to be measured and validated by that expression of the experience of faith.[12] For that reason, though the sermon shares in the process and power of Scripture, it remains subordinate and responsible to Scripture.

Yet the point remains that when the sermon results from responsible consideration of the new situation in the light of the traditions on the part of a respondent who comes from and acts for the community of faith, the power of God that inspired Scripture is again in contact with that community of faith. In such a way, a dynamic understanding of the inspiration of Scripture allows us to account for the historically demonstrated power of the proclaimed word to work its effects in the history of the church. Inspired Scripture is thus the invitation to continue to celebrate the presence of God with his people.

THE BELIEVING COMMUNITY

In all of this it is evident once more how closely Scripture is tied to the life of the community of faith. If, as we have seen, the nature of Scripture and the way we may understand it to be inspired is replicated in the continuing process of proclaiming the content of that Scripture, it is also true that one of the functions of Scripture is to be an invitation to join the pilgrimage of the community of faith, since according to the witness of that Scripture, the Spirit which inspired Scripture has come to dwell in the church. This also means that the appropriation of the experiences recorded in the Bible is to occur within that community where it can be shared and corrected by the way in which that experience is appropriated by fellow mem-

---

[12] See on this point John Goldingay, *Models for Scripture* (Grand Rapids: Eerdmans, 1994), 130.

bers of the community of faith.[13] Inspired Scripture which inspires in me the desire to shape my life in accord with its witness thus points me to the community of those who have been similarly inspired, where my appropriation of the biblical message can be corrected and the missing parts filled in by other members of that community. That is precisely the process Paul is describing in 1 Corinthians 12:4–11, and it serves as the model for the way the witness of inspired Scripture is to be appropriated.

Here again, the process of appropriating Scripture closely reflects the process by which Scripture came into existence. The traditions incorporated into our Scriptures represent the way generations within the community of faith, in Israel and in the church, sought to appropriate the experience of those who had gone before. If then there are inconsistencies in that record and in those traditions, it is precisely the inconsistencies that are reflections of the life of the community of faith. A life in the twentieth century that exactly replicated a life in the eighth century before Christ or the first century after Christ would not be a life of faith—it would be a grotesque anachronism. The Bible reflects the life of the faithful community over a span of centuries, and in the process of faithfully hearing and interpreting traditions in the light of new historical situations, the life of that community changed, and differed, from its earlier stages. Failure to change does not mean faithfulness, it means death, and a community which seeks to respond to a living God can hardly do so with an unchanging response that characterizes death rather than life.

That, further, means that the interpreter cannot be isolated from the community of faith. Insights must constantly be tested in and by the life of the community. To assume that the power of inspired Scripture is available in isolation from participation in that community is to deny the very nature of that Scripture, as we have seen it to be. It was for that reason, for example, that the Reformed tradition insisted on the rule of love as the principle of interpretation, by which it was meant that any interpretation of Scripture that did not promote love and brotherhood within the community needed to

---

[13] I have found useful here insights from MacKenzie, "The Social Character of Inspiration," 123; L. E. Keck, *The Problem of Biblical Authority* (circulated privately); Davis, *Debate About the Bible*, 76.

be reexamined.[14] If Scripture grew out of the community of faith, seeking both to confirm and to correct it, and if, therefore, Scripture is to be understood within that community of faith, then any understanding of Scripture that would finally be destructive of that community must be called into question. This cannot mean, of course, that only the interpretation which supports the status quo is to be accepted. On that test, no prophetic books would be in the canon. Yet it was precisely the purpose of the prophets to call the community of faith back to its true foundation, as it was the opposition of the false prophets that sought to defend the status quo. Valid interpretation can of course have as its goal the correction as well as the upbuilding of the community, but that interpretation which seeks wantonly to destroy the community of faith, or which is indifferent to its reality, is open to serious question, given the nature of the Scripture which is being interpreted.

NATURE OF BIBLICAL CONTENT

A further consequence to be drawn from the way we have sought to understand the origin of Scripture as the confluence of tradition, situation, and respondent, and to locate inspiration in that confluence, bears on the kind of material we can expect to find as a result. Clearly, as we have sought again and again to show, the intention of the biblical material is to summon the community of faith to a new awareness of its task and to a surer understanding of itself within God's purpose in new and often critical historical situations. That is, the intention of the material is religious rather than, say, historical or scientific. To ask, in those circumstances, that the biblical witness should anticipate late-twentieth-century views of science, or history, or geography, or any other kind of such information, is simply to miss the point of the nature of Scripture and the purpose of its inspiration. To seek another kind of truth in Scripture than the truth it intends to convey, let alone to make that other kind of truth the chief focus of investigation and apologetic, is as surely to pervert Scripture as is the wildest application

---

[14] I owe this insight to Leith, *Assembly at Westminster,* 80. The book as a whole is an excellent study of the Reformed ethos.

of the allegorical method. If the Bible has an intention other than to provide scientific knowledge, and it surely does, and if it has an intention other than to record events as would a modern positivistic historian, and it surely does, then to seek to find that kind of scientific or historical information is not only wrong, it is wrongheaded. Whatever the results of such investigative and apologetic efforts may be, they will be at best irrelevant, at worst destructive of the intention of Scripture.

The same judgment would have to apply to the expectation of inerrancy in all details, often associated with a search for scientific or historical truth which seeks to validate a certain view of inspiration, a view which, as we have seen, is at odds with the way Scripture was formed. Such minute inerrancy may be appropriate, even necessary, for a telephone book or the instruction manual for a computer, but not for psalms of rejoicing, or letters to recalcitrant communities of faith, or apocalyptic visions, or parables.[15] Similarly, "error" in that sense is an inappropriate category for the kind of Scripture we have.[16] The fundamental concept of truth in the Bible is not conformity between statement and "objective reality," but rather reliability, dependability. The opposite of such truth is not error, but fickleness or deliberate deception.[17] The real test of truth in Scripture is whether the respondent, confronted with a new situation, used the available traditions responsibly to encourage belief in the reliability of God and the dependability of his promises, not whether in some simile the figure happened to accord with what we take to be truth in the realm from which the simile was drawn.[18]

The same is true of historical statements. If, as some conservatives now feel compelled to concede, biblical authors used popular

---

[15] I owe the analogy of the telephone book to Rogers, ed., *Biblical Authority,* 67.

[16] As Goldingay (*Models for Scripture,* 280) points out, those "occasions when scriptures consciously speak approximately or profess ingorance (e.g., Luke 9:28; John 6:19; Acts 4:4; 2 Cor. 12:2; Rom. 15:24) indicate that inspiration did not make up for lack of ordinary human knowledge."

[17] On this point, see Vawter, *Biblical Inspiration,* 150–51, cf. also Barr, *Fundamentalism,* 55.

[18] This same point would apply to parables, which themselves are fiction, but which anyone familiar with the Christian faith will affirm, do in fact convey "truth." Thus truth is not exclusively congruent with "true facts." On this point see also B. S. Blaisdell, "A Liberal Response," in Charles R. Blaisdell, ed., *Conservative, Moderate, Liberal* (St. Louis, Mo.: CBP Press, 1990), 42.

views of science based on what people saw in the world around them, and hence, as observations, these descriptions were not in "error," then the same thing ought to be able to be said about history.[19] The same authors might well have used popular views of history which did not always accord with one another or with what we now are able to reconstruct of the situation. Yet again, such considerations are based on a view of the way Scripture was produced (the "prophetic model," in which an inspired individual wrote an entire book) that we have seen to be untenable in the light of our knowledge of the nature of the biblical materials. They are thus beside the point.

Yet there is also a deeper issue here. It is apparent that the historical traditions contained in the scriptural materials are not so much intent on reporting the past as they are on anticipating the future. History in the Bible is viewed from an eschatological angle of vision and is more interested in promises and their fulfillment than in sheer facticity of reporting. If history is the arena within which God is at work, a sheerly factual report would completely miss that dimension. What is at issue is not the number of troops in a battle, but the sweep of history within which that battle occurred, and what it portends for the future of the community of faith.[20] In those circumstances, to be perturbed when reports of chariots or infantry disagree in numbers is to miss the mountain range while trying to account for the pebble. The intention of Scripture is to witness to realities larger than minute numerical accuracy.

THE CRITICAL METHOD IN BIBLE STUDY

If the inspiration of Scripture is to be understood as we have described it, that has implications not only for the kind of content we are to seek but also for the way we are to seek it. We are aware how in a variety of times (freedom and captivity, war and peace, poverty and prosperity) and of forms (prophecy and history, devotional materials

---

[19] Vawter, *Biblical Inspiration,* 122, has made this point as well.

[20] As William C. Placher ("The Nature of Biblical Authority: Issues and Models from Recent Theology," in Blaisdell, ed., *Conservative, Moderate, Liberal,* 13) points out, the point of a story is not the truth of its details but its invitation to us to see the world in its terms and to enter into a relationship with the God of whom it speaks.

and apocalyptic visions, Gospels and epistles) God has, through his Holy Spirit, summoned forth from the confluence of situations, traditions, and respondents a witness to his will and to his purposes for his people. Because that is the process by which Scripture has been formed, the witness it bears is a true witness. That is, it is a witness understandable to the people to whom it was originally addressed. That means the witness is time-bound. Addressed to a specific situation in the light of specific traditions by a respondent or respondents who were immersed in that situation, the witness will be given in terms of the world view in which those realities have meaning. Because world views and situations change, traditions must be interpreted anew and the witness given anew. That is the nature of true witness, as it is the nature of Scripture. Unless the witness borne is understandable to those to whom it is borne, it is not a true witness.

All of that is to say that in Scripture the witness of God to his people has become human discourse. Those respondents who contributed to the shaping of tradition, who proclaimed those reshaped traditions, and who finally recorded them, were all people limited to the historical and cultural context within which they worked. In significant ways, that cultural situation was different from ours. That in its turn has two implications. One, the witness must be addressed anew, in a situation similar to the construction of that witness through the confluence of traditions, situation, and respondent, in the form of the proclamation of that witness to the contemporary community of faith. We have already explored that implication. The second implication is in a sense the presupposition of the first: in order for our contemporary witness to be faithful to the intention of that original witness, we must discern what that intention was. If that intention was aimed at a cultural situation other than the one which we inhabit (and it was), then to understand that witness, we must understand all we can of that other cultural situation out of which, and for which, the witness was framed. We must know something of the shape of the traditions prior to that witness, so we can better comprehend the significance of the changed emphases in the witness to the new situation. We must know something of that new situation, if we are to understand the point of the change in emphasis. We must also know something of the way in which ideas were expressed, the thought and language forms available, the customs of literary expression, and the conventions of communication. In short, we must know what modes of communication were available to the respondents who shaped the traditions for the new situation.[21]

The attempt to gain such knowledge impels what are called the "critical" studies of the Bible. Far from seeking to discredit Scripture, the motive of such critical studies is simply to come to a better understanding of the situation into which the witness was given, so we may better understand that witness. We must seek to know how traditions change their shape and destiny from biblical book to biblical book, to see the intention of the new shape in the new time. Ignorant of the shift if we do not know something of the original shape of the tradition, how can we discern the new word that God would speak through his Holy Spirit to that new situation? Ignorant of the situation into which God addresses his word through his Spirit, how can we know something of the point those reshaped traditions wanted to make? Ignorant of linguistic and literary conventions, how can we distinguish between the respondent's speaking or writing in the way that all his or her contemporaries normally wrote to make a conventional point and when a respondent bent old forms or created new ones to express God's witness to his will in that new time? Historical-critical work on the text of the Bible is therefore not an attempt to obscure the clear witness of Scripture, but rather an attempt to listen to its witness in a disciplined way, so that we do not impose our modern prejudices upon that ancient word of God to his people. If we hear only what we already know from Scripture, what profit is that for us, in what way is that the word of God to us? Yet if we are not aware of cultural and linguistic differences, how can we hear anything but familiar things, in that case familiar because they have been distorted by the modern frame of reference we bring to those ancient accounts?[22]

---

[21] This point is made in paradigmatic fashion in par. 12 of the *Constitution on Divine Revelation*: to understand Scripture's intention, "Due attention must be paid to the customary and characteristic styles of perceiving, speaking and narrating which prevailed at the time of the sacred writer, and to the customs men normally followed at that period in their everyday dealings with one another."

[22] The absence of such emphases in the creeds of the time of the Reformation is nicely accounted for by Leith, *Assembly at Westminster,* 79, when he points out that "there is a far deeper gulf between the last third of the twentieth century and the world of the Westminster Assembly than there was between the world of the

Modern scholars must therefore exercise the greatest care in their study of literary forms so that they can recognize what that form would communicate to its hearers. To assume that a metaphor common in the ancient world is meant to be a literal description of truth could only lead to a distortion of what that witness attempted to say. Not to know that a prophetic oracle assumes a legal form when the prophet wants to call attention to the rupture of God's law is to miss part of the witness of that oracle to its time. Not to know what elements were essential to reporting a miracle in the Hellenistic world is to miss the theological interpretations the tradition has built into those stories for our understanding of their several intentions. For that reason, the critical study of literary forms is essential to an understanding of inspired Scripture constructed from such forms.[23]

Modern scholars must exercise the greatest care in their study of the historical events into which the biblical witness was spoken. Not to know the kind of threat represented by some world empire or another, or to be ignorant of the way such empires treated subjected people, condemns us to a partial understanding at best of what a historical report or prophetic oracle sought to convey to people who were aware of such things. To be ignorant of the dynamics within the Roman Empire, and the relationship of provinces to one another, condemns us to a muddled understanding of some of the allusions in Paul's letters. Not to know precisely what the intention of the Pharisaic legal exegesis was, or the loyalties of the Sadducees, or the dreams and ambitions of the Zealots, is to condemn ourselves to a sheerly superficial understanding of the power of Jesus' words and acts among such people. For that reason a careful study of the situation out of which, and for which, a given scriptural witness was formed is essential for understanding inspired Scripture.

Westminster Assembly and that of the New Testament," and for that reason critical studies are more obviously necessary to us than to people of that period. Leith comments: "This new cultural situation reveals inadequacies in the method by which the writers of the [Westminster] Confession moved from the Holy Scripture to the contemporary situation that were not obvious to the wise and able theologians of the seventeenth century." That same insight is valid throughout the period of Reformation creedal writing.

[23] This point is also implied in the Vatican II statement cited in n. 15.

Care must also be given to determining the time in which the various biblical witnesses were fixed, if we are to know how the world appeared to the various respondents, and how therefore we are to understand their reactions to it, as they shaped older traditions to meet new situations. Unless we can appreciate the limits and opportunities offered by the intellectual world they inhabited, we stand a good chance of missing the intention of their response to the impulse of the Holy Spirit in their situation.

The greatest care must therefore be taken in the attempt to understand as closely as possible the three components of Scripture (tradition, situation, and respondent) in order to understand what they intended to say to their world, so that we may apply that insight correctly to our time. In that fashion we, like the respondents of old, exercise care in understanding the traditions we have been given, so that, faithful to the impulse of the Holy Spirit, we may discern and proclaim God's will for our time. Holy Scripture represents the tradition to which we as respondents must react, lay and clergy alike, in our ever-new situations. Critical study of that tradition seeks to be as faithful to that tradition in our time as were the respondents who shaped that Scripture to the traditions they received in their time. In that way modern students of Scripture may be as faithful to the call of God through his Spirit to witness to his will in our time as were those who shaped the authoritative form of the traditions given to us in our Bible.

Some objections to critical studies indicate a complete misunderstanding of their nature and subject matter. It is argued, for instance, that one cannot suppose the hearers of Hosea had all the scholarly equipment and knowledge of a modern Old Testament scholar, yet they understood the message, and the implication is that we should be able to as well. That argument overlooks the fact that what Hosea's hearers knew as children of their age and culture which they shared with Hosea, we can know only through painstaking historical reconstruction. The point is that as modern Western people who speak English, we can know what Hosea's hearers knew automatically—language, customs, historical situation—only by careful historical study. We must do all that simply to get to the place where Hosea's hearers were as a matter of their birth and upbringing.

Again, some want to argue that the work of critical scholars makes the Bible appear so complex that a simple reader could not possibly understand Scripture without considerable help. The implication is, since such scholarly endeavor uncovers complexity, it ought to be abandoned. That would be similar to arguing that since modern physics has shown our world to be incredibly complex, from subatomic particles to the "big bang" theory of the origin of the universe, it ought to be abandoned. Otherwise how can simple people understand the universe in which they live? In fact, many people who live in the universe do have a distorted idea of what it is like. The same is true of the Bible. If it is a complex phenomenon, as modern scholarship has shown it to be, then one can hardly for that reason abandon such scholarship. People also have many and distorted views of Scripture, which critical studies can help to dispel. That of course is why most churches require their clergy to be specially trained. If the Bible could be understood perfectly by anyone even without such training, why educate ministers? The need for continually deeper education of the clergy shows the inadequacy of such argumentation. To continue to affirm a view of the Bible framed in the eighteenth century in the face of modern critical methods and discoveries is comparable to someone affirming Newtonian physics in the post-Einstein period. Both are misguided to the point of being grotesque. Critical studies have been made necessary by the sheer complexity of the phenomenon under investigation, and no amount of pious rhetoric or fiery attacks can change that fact. As we have seen, critical studies are made necessary by the nature of the Bible and are needed to get at the intention of its material. There is more distortion of Scripture without such studies than there is as a result of them.

FURTHER THEOLOGICAL PROBLEMS

Our investigation of the nature of the Bible, and of the way in which inspiration is to be understood as a result, has some implications for the question of the unity of the Bible as well.

That the reality to which Scripture points is described in differing, at times even incompatible, ways is the natural outcome of the process by which, as we have seen, Scripture came into existence. As situations change, former acts of God take on new meanings, and hence the traditions are adapted to bear the freight of that new meaning. A unitary outlook on the reality of God would be possible only if the Bible were produced by a group of like-minded people writing to a group of like-minded people over a short period of time. Such a Bible would have relevance only for that group during that short period of time. Rather, the Bible is the result of the earnest search for God's will for his world in ever-changing situations, and the mark of the faithfulness of the respondents to the living traditions of God's acts in the past is seen precisely in the differing interpretations given to those acts in the differing situations faced by the various respondents. The final unity of the Bible will not occur until the final act of God with and for his people has been completed, something which the community of faith affirms is not yet the case. Until that time, the Bible represents a fragmentary understanding of the "ways of God with men and women," and its unity must be found in the source of the traditions of which it is composed, namely, God himself.

That same reality of which we learn from the witness of Scripture is also the basis of the certainty of a faith nourished and sustained by that witness. Such certainty of faith cannot be derived from any kind of prior assumption we feel it necessary to bring to Scripture, to satisfy our need for certainty. The assumptions we bring can only provide us with a certainty that we ourselves can achieve through the establishment of such assumptions, and it is precisely the certainty beyond what we can attain for ourselves that is at issue in biblical faith. When inerrantists claim that rejection of assumptions about inerrancy of detail deprives us of the certainty which in fact only trust in God can bring, they confuse human assertion with divine truth. That fault is continually illustrated in the messages of the false prophets. It is precisely the imposition of our ideas upon the word of God that is the chief source of uncertainty about his will. The basis for certainty lies not in the *form* of Scripture, but in its *content,* and any attempt to give more importance to the former will in the end work counter to a certainty of faith. Assumptions about inerrancy that provoke desperate defenses and uncharitable attacks on those who disagree can hardly be a useful basis for the certainty of faith. Such certainty must be found in the God to whom Scripture points, or it will not be found at all. Scripture is surely our most useful instrument in attaining such certainty, but to confuse the form of the witness that Scripture brings with the true source of certainty—God alone—can result only in uncertainty and the despairing attempts to combat it which characterize much conservative apologetic about the nature of that scriptural witness.

Such reflections also point to the relationship between the revelation of God's will and the scriptural witness to that will. While Scripture is our only source of knowledge of the way God made his will known in the past, it nevertheless consistently points away from itself in speaking of that will. To identify the form of the scriptural witness to God's will with the revelation of that will, as though God's will were now identical with and imprisoned within the inerrant form of that witness, imprisoned within an understanding of the natural world we can no longer share, is to deny the continuing power of the internal testimony of the Holy Spirit to use Scripture to illumine God's will for us. Through that testimony of the Holy Spirit, the Bible can again become for us a living witness to God's will and thus can become the instrument of revelation to us. Apart from that testimony, received with an open and willing heart, Scripture remains mute, as its rejection by many in the modern world makes clear. God continues to be selective in the revelation of his will, as he was in the history of Israel and in the foundation of the church. Not all events in the history of Israel revealed God's will. The emergence of false prophets, who thought they discerned such revelatory events, but did not, bears witness to that fact. It is only the true prophetic witness that allows us to recognize which events in Israel's history are in fact revelatory of the will of Israel's God. That prophetic witness is then concretized in the Old Testament scriptural witness to those events, and to that prophetic identification. Not every event in the first century of our era was revelatory of God's will for humankind. Only the career, death, and resurrection of Jesus of Nazareth carried such revelatory freight, and it was the prophetic office of the apostles that allows us to recognize in those events the culminating revelation of God's will for his world. That prophetic witness is then also concretized in the New Testament scriptural witness to that event and to that prophetic identification. But in each instance, Old and New Testament Scripture points away from itself, and to key events, as the locus of revelation. If Scripture, through the internal testimony of the Holy Spirit, can function for us as the revelation of the will of God for us, and for his world, it functions as such a witness to events outside itself, in which we may discern the intention of that divine will.

It is further the case that it is the message of Scripture alone that leads one to find in it a reality which illumines life and gives meaning to human society. The reliability of Scripture is to be found in the reality to which it points, rather than the form in which it is given. Respect for the gospel, for example, is shown by hearing and trusting its content, not in involved apologetics designed to show that the Gospel accounts are only fragmentary reports of a larger reality, as when it is affirmed that Peter really denied Jesus six times, but that the Gospels show only parts of that event. The gospel is not served with such attention to the details of its response to the situation faced by the respondents who gave to the traditions the form they now have. Accounts differ because the situations for which the respondents shaped them differed, and that fact must be respected.

The "proof" of the inspiration of Scripture, similarly, lies not in any prior categories which can be applied to it, which would guarantee that God's Spirit was at work in its formation. Rather, the demonstration of the inspiration of Scripture is to be seen in the effects the Bible has produced within humankind by means of the use of Scripture in and by the community of faith. There is no way one can be sure that the Bible is inspired save to subject oneself to the Lord to whom that Scripture points. No appeal to inerrancy, or unity, or historical reliability can spare an individual from committing his or her life to the Lord to whom the Bible witnesses. To the one who thus commits life, however, no further proofs for the authority or inspiration of Scripture are necessary. It is precisely the trustworthiness of the witness of Scripture, proved in the life of the community of faith, that has led the church to speak of the "inspiration" of certain of the books produced by Israel and the Christian community, and to include them in its canon.

It is therefore trust in the Lord of Scripture that has led to formulations of the inspired nature of the writings. It is the confirmation of the rightness of that trust that has led to formulations of the reliability of the words of Scripture. It is the message of Scripture, overwhelming in its power to transform the lives of the faithful through the power of the Spirit, that leads us to trust its reliability and to seek to express that reliability in terms of its inspiration by that same Spirit.[24] Surely writings that are so clearly used by the Spirit in the

---

[24] I owe this formulation to Berkouwer, *Holy Scripture,* 264.

work of God must also have shared in the power of that Spirit in their creation. It is that insight that is the root of the doctrine of the inspiration of Scripture,[25] and it is the attempt to formulate that doctrine in a manner commensurate with the way in which those Scriptures came into existence that has occupied us in the pages of this book. It is precisely in the dynamic situation of the Lord of history creating and revealing himself to the community of faith that Scripture was born, being summoned forth from the confluence of tradition, situation, and respondent. It is in the dynamic work of the Spirit that the inspired nature of those Scriptures has proved itself again and again to the community of faith as that community has sought to shape its life in accordance with the will of God.

If, as we saw earlier, the Bible is silent on the question of its own inerrancy and remarkably reticent in statements about its own nature, it bears a continuing and unabating witness to the presence of God with the community of faith, shaping and guiding its life as it confronted the ever-changing situations of new historical times. Since it is precisely out of that continual guidance that, we have urged, we are to find the locus of the inspiration of Scripture, there is ample evidence for that kind of inspiration. There is no need to seek to press out of scriptural passages statements about the nature of Scripture those passages were never intended to bear. Rather, the witness of Scripture from beginning to end points to the reality out of which Scripture grew and within which we are to find its inspiration, namely, the continuing guidance of the community of faith by God's Spirit. On that way of understanding the nature of scriptural inspiration the Scripture is not silent. It is, in fact, the very content of its witness from creation to final consummation.

---

[25] Luke Johnson ("The Authority of the NT in the Church: A Theological Reflection," in Blaisdell, ed., *Conservative, Moderate, Liberal,* 90–91) put the matter nicely: "The ecclesial decision to regard these writings as Scripture bears with it the recognition that they have a peculiar and powerful claim on the lives of individuals and above all on the community as a whole. . . . Divine inspiration is one of the ways of expressing the unique authority Christians attribute to these writings."

Chapter 7

The Authority of
Inspired Scripture

The link we have sought to establish between the inspiration of Scripture and the formation of the canon, with the canon helping to identify which writings of the early church are uniquely inspired, leads directly to the question of the authority of Scripture, since both canon and inspiration point to, and help define, that authority. In this final chapter we need to examine, if only briefly, some aspects that are useful in any consideration of biblical authority.

THE LOCUS OF AUTHORITY

To raise the question of authority within a context of the canonical collection of inspired Scripture is to be pointed by that entity not to itself and the documents of which it is comprised, but rather to be pointed to One who lies beyond the documents, and from whom the documents derive such authority as they have. To ask the canonical Scripture about authority is to be pointed to Christ, and thus to be pointed beyond Christ to the One who acted in him to redeem and judge the world.

The Jesus who speaks and acts in the Gospels does so with sovereign authority over people, over forces of evil, and over nature itself. Yet one cannot read the Gospels without being struck by the fact that their central character, Jesus of Nazareth, points beyond himself to the God whom he calls "Father" and who exercises control over his fate (e.g., Mark 14:36). That fatherhood, and implicitly the control over his fate, are confirmed by the heavenly voice in those events where he finds divine legitimation: his baptism and his Transfiguration. The final legitimation that points beyond Jesus to the One who sent him is shown in his resurrection from the dead by means of the divine power.

That Jesus points beyond himself to God is then also acknowledged implicitly by those who observe his deeds and give expression to the wonder they call forth. Responses like those to the expelled demon—"with authority he commands even the unclean spirits" (Mark 1:27)—and to the stilled storm on the sea of Galilee—"Who then is this, that even wind and sea obey him?" (Mark 4:41)—are examples of finding in Jesus things that point beyond him to a source of authority exceeding that normally found in human beings.

The same is true of the epistles. Paul regularly points away from himself to Christ as the locus of his authority. It is Christ to whom he owes his very life as an apostle (Phil. 3:7–11) and who is the exhaustive content of his proclamation (1 Cor. 2:2). Even his appeals to his own apostolic authority are predicated on the content to which such apostolic authority points. Apart from the risen Christ, Paul knows himself to be nothing and to have no authority at all. Thus, Paul's own apostolic authority consists precisely in pointing away from himself to the authority of the one whom he proclaims.

In doing this, Paul is paradigmatic of the authority possessed by all Scripture. That authority is to be found in God's act in Christ, to which the Old Testament points in anticipation and which the New Testament summons to remembrance. For that reason, differences in the way that sayings of Jesus were remembered or events were retold, or discrepancies in the reporting of events in the Old Testament books which concern the fate of Israel, do not compromise the authority of that record. The biblical record cannot supplant the authority of the living God, but draws its authority from its reflection of his reality, a reality which is recalled in Scripture, but which is recalled as an event in history, in time and space. That reality of God and of his acts is subject to reporting, reflection, application, and interpretation in our Bible, as the community of faith sought and seeks to come to terms with what it means to live in a universe created, sustained, and ruled by the God who chose for himself a people and then a church.

Because the authority of Scripture lies not in itself but in the living God to whom it points, such authority is not confined to the past but continues in the present. Because God speaks through the Scriptures to the community he has called into existence, the authority of those Scriptures is a continuing authority, summoning those who read it to hear and obey the voice of the God to whom it points.[1]

It is clear from all this that the authority of the Scripture is a derived authority. It is in the final analysis not the text that matters, but the one to whom that text points.[2] And that in its turn means that the authority of Scripture lies in its content, and more specifically in its content as witness to the God to whom it points. Scripture functions authoritatively when it functions as witness, pointing beyond itself to the reality of God as the final locus of truth. Scripture does not function authoritatively when it is understood as pointing to itself as the source of inerrant truth, because at that point it has given up its primary function as witness to a reality beyond itself. That the authority of Scripture lies in its content also means that its authority is not derived from the community that collected and preserved the traditions, nor from the institution that collected the books and formed them into a canon. Finally, if the content is the locus of authority, one cannot locate the authority in reconstructed traditions that may underlie the books of the Bible as we now have them, such as a hypothetical "Q" document.[3] Nor can authority reside in any reconstruction of the "real Jesus" that appeals to material beyond the content of Scripture, correcting the supposed "false" picture of Jesus constructed by the church from its canonical Scripture. Nor can scriptural authority be assigned to any experience claimed to be derived from a reading of the content of that Scripture, however that experience may express itself, and however laudable its goals may appear.[4] The authority of Scripture functions not to validate human experience, however derived; rather Scripture functions authoritatively when it creates and

---

[1] On this point, see Abraham, *Divine Inspiration*, 51; Marshall, *Biblical Inspiration*, 125; Bloesch, *Holy Scripture*, 125.

[2] So also e.g., Goldingay, *Models for Scripture*, 77.

[3] "Q" is the name given to an imagined source that is assumed to have furnished the material that Matthew and Luke have in common that they did not derive from Mark.

[4] David M. Scholer ("The Nature of Biblical Authority: A Moderate Perspective," in Charles R. Blaisdell, ed., *Conservative, Moderate, Liberal* [St. Louis, Mo.: CBP Press, 1990], 61) makes this point well; he identifies some attempts of liberation and feminist theologies as attempts to locate authority in the reader or the reader's experience.

corrects the experience of those who read its words, shaping that experience in terms of the reality to which it bears witness.

The power that enables Scripture to create and correct human experience is precisely the divine power that underlies the shaping of Scripture itself, namely the Holy Spirit. Because the locus of authority lies beyond the text itself, and inheres in the God to whom Scripture points, such authority can function only when that same divine power is at work in the one who reads and hears the witness of Scripture. Apart from the power of the Holy Spirit, Scripture lies dumb at best, or is used in a misleading way at worst.

Yet it is also the case that the witness of the Holy Spirit is not heard apart from the content of the witness contained in the text. It is precisely the claim that the Holy Spirit can be heard apart from the text that leads to the kind of aberrations mentioned above, however reverently that claim may be made. Some have claimed, for example, that one limits the power of the Holy Spirit to confront people outside the confines of Scripture[5] when one makes the content of the scriptural witness the sole source of Christian faith and practice. Yet detaching the witness of the Holy Spirit from the Scriptures, themselves inspired by that same Holy Spirit, is to open the gates to all manner of subjective, not to say self-interested, religious claims. It is also unnecessary, since one would not expect self-contradiction from the Holy Spirit, which would rule out any "revelation" or content from that Spirit which differed in any significant way from the Scriptures. The need to test such "inspiration" by the Holy Spirit, to see whether or not it conforms to the self-witness of God given in Scripture, is noted already in that witness, when the author of 1 John admonishes his readers to test the spirit, to see whether it be of God (1 John 4:1). Unless the claim that the Holy Spirit is speaking through the individual and the church is subordinate to the authority of the biblical witness, individual and church are at the mercy of subjective opinion.[6]

It is just this claim of inspiration by the Holy Spirit apart from the witness of Scripture that has led to the loss of biblical authority

---

[5] This is the claim, for example, of Gloria Tate, "A Moderate Response," in Charles R. Blaisdell, ed., *Conservative, Moderate, Liberal* (St. Louis, Mo.: CBP Press, 1990), 54, who argues that to depend on the Bible alone "allows no room for the creative work of the Holy Spirit that generates revelation."

[6] So also Marshall, *Biblical Inspiration,* 121.

within the liberal view. Over against the claim that because the witness of Scripture stands in a unique relationship to the God who inspired it, that witness is authoritative, the notion gained currency that because men are the authors of the biblical witness, that witness has no intrinsic authority beyond that of any other human writing.[7] The loss of the authoritative biblical witness has thus meant the substitution of the authoritative voices in any given cultural situation. To lose the authority of the biblical witness is to become captive to the culture and its ruling norms, a point repeatedly demonstrated by both the radical right and the radical left in modern political life. The Christian community that abandons the authority of the biblical witness becomes little more than the mouthpiece of whatever current cultural norms catch its fancy.

BIBLICAL AUTHORITY AND FAITH

If the testimony of the Holy Spirit is essential to a recognition of the inspiration and hence the authority of the biblical witness, such recognition is and remains open to faith alone. To be sure, features of the Bible point to its inspiration and authority: its high moral teachings, its fulfilled prophecies, the great literature its witness has produced. Yet other features point in the opposite direction: unresolved historical problems embodied within the narratives, ethically questionable statements and commands, confusion of detail in reporting the same events.[8] Thus, in the end, it is a matter of faith whether or not one accepts the idea of the divine inspiration and authority of the biblical witness, to be sure a faith itself prompted by the inspiration of the same Holy Spirit who points to the truth of the scriptural witness.[9] For that reason the Bible is accepted as authoritative in communities of faith, both Jewish and Christian, as part of their confession of faith.[10]

---

[7] A point also made by Berkeley Mickelsen, "The Bible's Own Approach to Authority," in Jack Rogers, ed., *Biblical Authority* (Waco, Tex.: Word Books, 1977), 78.

[8] On this point see also Marshall, *Biblical Inspiration,* 46.

[9] On this point see also Marshall, *Biblical Inspiration,* 51, 121, and Rogers, "The Church Doctrine of Biblical Authority," 27, who quotes Calvin to the same effect.

[10] See on this point Scholer, "The Nature of Biblical Authority," 58.

Yet some who want to affirm the authority of the biblical witness find such an identification of the recognition of that authority with a confession of faith to be unsatisfactory. So important a doctrine of the Christian faith must, in their view, have a solider base that simply a confession of faith, which itself is open to the charge of being subjective. Instead of finding the central locus of the authority of the biblical witness in the faith of the confessing community, that authority is found in the general concept of the authority of truth.

Thus the authority of the specific biblical witness is subordinated to the authority of truth of any kind; biblical truth is thus a subset of truth as an overarching concept. So, it is argued, any true statement has the right to compel belief and action. It is therefore because the Bible is true that it has such authority.[11]

Yet truth is an elusive concept. In order to define it more strictly, this view argues that truth consists in correspondence with reality. Such truth, admittedly, is a property only of propositions, i.e., statements, affirmations, indicative sentences.[12] In its turn, such a view of truth, and of the authority of the biblical witness dependent on it, makes logically inevitable the claim for the propositional nature of the truth of the biblical witness.[13]

In sum, the Bible is authoritative on this view because it is true, and that truth is demonstrated by the unity of the Bible, by its fulfilled prophecies, by its remarkable accuracy determined by archaeological and historical investigation, and by the internal consistency of its statements.[14] As a result, those who hold this position can argue that they do not accept the authority of the Bible blindly, i.e., by faith, but use their reason to identify and verify it as the word of God and thus the embodiment of divine authority.[15]

It is because the divine authority of the Bible consists in propositional truth that such propositions must be without error, i.e.,

---

[11] Why the Bible is then more authoritative than any other true statement witnessing to God's involvement in human affairs, or to the centrality of the Christ event, as in, say, Augustine's *City of God,* is not clear.

[12] How this comports with the scriptural injunction to do the truth (John 3:21) as well as know it (John 8:32) is not discussed.

[13] I am reflecting here the arguments of Cottrell, "The Nature of Biblical Authority," 23–24.

[14] So Cottrell, "The Nature of Biblical Authority," 23.

[15] Cottrell, "The Nature of Biblical Authority," 34–35.

inerrant, or they would not be true, since truth and error are mutually exclusive. Yet when errors, i.e., statements that contradict one another, or are in "tension" with one another, and hence make it impossible for both propositions to be true, are in fact identified, such "tensions" are attributed, as a last resort, to the process of copying the original manuscripts. The original manuscripts, the "autographs," on the other hand, were in fact error-free, on this view. As has often been pointed out, however, those autographs are unavailable to us. As a result, one cannot verify the truth of the proposition that the autographs were inerrant. Acceptance of their inerrancy is thus an article of faith, not demonstration or verification. In the end, therefore, the final demonstration of the authority of the scriptural witness is an article of faith. Thus those who argue for the authority of truth reasonably established also end on an affirmation of faith: truth was exclusively the property of the text of the unseen and unverifiable autographs.

The dispute between those who acknowledge that the truth of the witness of Scripture, confirmed by the Holy Spirit, is an article of faith, and those who affirm the final truth of unavailable autographs, is not a dispute between faith and reason, as it were, but a dispute between competing articles of faith. Whatever one may want to conclude about the appropriateness of such competing faiths, one must finally acknowledge that in fact, however it may be phrased and defended, the affirmation of the authority of the biblical witness is a matter of faith and needs to be debated and discussed on that basis.

IDENTIFICATION OF BIBLICAL AUTHORITY

The question underlying the debate between those who argue for an inerrant text, even if only in the autographs, and those who locate the authority of Scripture in the work of the Holy Spirit verifiable only to faith—that question concerns the way in which the authority of Scripture may be demonstrated. In the last analysis, to find that authority located in the literary form in which the scriptural witness has been cast, i.e., in its inerrant, original though unavailable form, is to locate the authority beyond the reach of reality. Yet in fact historically the reality of the authority of Scripture can be seen to lie not in its literary form, but in the reality to which that literary form has given rise.

On the most basic level, the authority of Scripture lies in its ability to *author* reality, that is, to create a certain identity previously nonexistent in those who hear its witness, and to bring into existence, and subsequently to renew, the fellowship of persons in whom such new identity has been "authored," namely, the Christian community.[16] Such authority thus transforms the vision of reality of those who acknowledge it. It calls such persons to a different vision of things, discrepant to the dominant ethos of the surrounding culture.[17] The witness of Scripture accomplishes that by the fact that Christians do not then find their own stories confirmed in Scripture, but make the scriptural story and its witness their own and allow it to transform their own stories. They do not translate Scripture into categories familiar and comfortable to them and their surrounding society, but rather they translate and understand their own experience by means of the categories furnished by the scriptural witness. Such authority therefore cannot be the property of or controlled by any Christian community or its leadership. Rather the authority of the scriptural witness manifests itself by its transformative power worked on the whole of that Christian community.[18]

The authority of Scripture is therefore demonstrated, not in the literary form in which it has been cast, as supporters of inerrancy would have it, but rather in its power to create and shape reality. It is the experience of the community of faith with the Bible that gives the basis for the confession of the authority of that Bible. Those writings have authority because it has been the experience of the church over centuries that God uses the words contained in them to carry on his work of sanctifying sinful people. The authority of Scripture is therefore not found in any formula that can be applied to them, nor in any prior conception of what God's word would have to be if it were to be

---

[16] I owe the use of the word *author* in this context to Luke Johnson, "The Authority of the NT in the Church: A Theological Reflection," in Charles R. Blaisdell, ed., *Conservative, Moderate, Liberal* (St. Louis, Mo.: CBP Press, 1990), 94.

[17] On this point see W. C. Placher, "The Nature of Biblical Authority," in Charles R. Blaisdell, ed., *Conservative, Moderate, Liberal* (St. Louis, Mo.: CBP Press, 1990), 4.

[18] I am indebted here to the insights of Goldingay, *Models for Scripture*, 109; Bloesch, *Holy Scripture*, 160.

God's word (i.e., inerrant, noncontradictory of modern notions, etc.), but rather in the life-transforming power that those words have demonstrated in the life of the community of faith.

That community of faith did not create the life-transforming power of the reality to which the Scripture bears witness, however, and hence has not created the authority of that witness. The authority of the Scriptures is not created, but is recognized, by the church. It is that act of recognition that is also shown in the formation of the Christian canon, to which we must now turn our attention.

CANON AND SCRIPTURAL AUTHORITY

The canon, as is the case with Scripture, is the result of the reflection and experience of the Christian community, although the assembly of the canon took longer and as a result has left a clearer historical trail of its process of assembly than the similar process by which the New Testament Scriptures reached their final form. There is another difference between the realities of canon and Scripture, in addition to the visibility and transparency of their processes of assembly, however. In the case of the canon, the Christian community, on the basis of several hundred years of experience with its sacred writings, eventually recognized which of those writings were to have decisive, i.e., canonical, significance. scriptural traditions, and indeed the New Testament Scriptures themselves, on the other hand, and the reality to which they witness, existed prior to the existence of the Christian community in any form in which it could assemble and recognize a canon of Scripture. On that basis, it appears that while New Testament Scripture, and the traditions it contains, created the Christian community, that community, on the other hand, created the canon. Yet like Scripture, the canon and the authority which inheres in it, are based ultimately on the recognition rather than the creation of that authority.

In the assembly and recognition of the canon, therefore, the Christian community acknowledges the authority of the scriptural witness to the realities upon which that community is based and which called it into existence. By being acknowledged in that way as the authoritative witness to the foundational events of the Christian community, the canon itself becomes a part of those foundational events. As a part of those foundational events, the canon possesses an authority which can no more be ignored or bypassed than the witness to the foundational events the canon contains within itself. The continuing existence of the Christian community, and the acknowledgement of the authority of the canon, are therefore inseparable.

The authority of the canon thus acknowledged exercises itself within the Christian community by means of a hermeneutical function:[19] by containing the authoritative witness to the foundational events of the Christian community, it also defines the range of appropriate interpretations of the foundational events of the Christian faith. The canon represents and contains within its writings the source and content of the authoritative witness to its foundational events, within which the witness and proclamation of the Christian community find the basis of such activity. Thus the content and the proclamation of Christian faith and life are found in their authoritative form within the writings contained in the canon.

In addition to pointing to the content of the authoritative and hence trustworthy witness to the foundational events, there is another, equally important, way in which the canon performs its hermeneutical function. The canon also functions hermeneutically by placing limits on both the content and the form the witness and proclamation of those foundational events may take. The canon thus functions in a sense as a boundary marker, displaying at which points an interpretation of the Christian faith has abandoned a legitimate understanding of the faith's foundational events.

An illustration of this function can be found in Scripture itself. When the author of 1 John warns his readers to test the various spirits at work in the church so as to be able to discern those that come from God, and hence, by implication, those that are authoritative and trustworthy, and those that are false, and hence deceitful and untrustworthy, the test he provides is the form and content of the incarnation of Christ. Any spirit which prompts to the confession that Christ has truly come in the flesh can confidently be trusted as coming from God. Any spirit, however, that does not prompt the confession that

---

[19] The following reflections on the hermeneutical function of the canon were prompted by some comments of Professor Peter Stuhlmacher, contained in private correspondence.

Christ has truly come in the flesh is false, and is to be ignored. Any witness, therefore, to the Christ event which does not reflect the actual incarnation of Christ is false and is not to be tolerated within the Christian community. In this instance, the incarnation functions as the *rule* (the meaning of the Greek word *kanōn*) for the faith of the church. It is this interpretative function that the canon also exercises on a broader scale for the Christian community at large. Any confession, or proclamation, or way of life that does not comport with the authoritative witness contained within the writings of the canon is deceitful and inherently untrustworthy.

While the hermeneutical or interpretative function of the canon in providing the content of the faith and proclamation of the Christian community has often been emphasized, the limiting aspect of the canon has not always been similarly recognized or equally valued. Yet that limiting interpretative function must also be taken seriously, because it is importantly in that limiting mode that the canon effectively exercises its function of interpretative context. The limiting function exercised by the canon is in fact of equal hermeneutical importance because in its very existence as a collection of diverse writings, the canon does not give the kind of unanimous witness that would be necessary for it to function exclusively in a positive way, as an indication of content. To ignore the hermeneutical function of limiting and to look to the canon only in its mode of defining content is to expect to find a total and unitary form of content which the canon does not provide, despite the best attempts of those who see it in that mode to make it comply with such a form.[20] Rather, the witness of the canon functions, perhaps most importantly, to exclude interpretations of the foundational events of the community of faith which do not comport with the canonical witness to the faith's foundational events. Excluded, for example, is an understanding of the exodus of Israel from Egypt that would interpret it as having occurred as the result purely of socio-political forces, entirely apart from the intention of God for his people Israel. Similarly excluded is an understanding of Jesus' death that would interpret it as having occurred solely to atone

---

[20] It is the failure of the inerrantists to recognize the importance of this inherently limiting function of the canon that causes them to seek to find, and even to create, a unitary witness to the foundational events which reaches into the smallest details of all aspects of its content.

for his own sins, or that would interpret the resurrection of Jesus of Nazareth from the dead as though it did not occur by the power of God, or in full accord with the divine will. If the canon does not prescribe in minute and unanimous detail how those events are to be interpreted, it does set the limits within which those interpretations may be regarded as valid and hence authoritative. It is in that important hermeneutical function that the canon finds and exercises its authority for the life and proclamation of the Christian community. It is this hermeneutical function of limitation that is frequently denied in our present culture both within and outside of the confessing Christian community.

The attempt to find authoritative interpretations of the life and teaching of Jesus apart from the canonical limitations is one expression of this denial. The boundaries of the canon are simply considered too limiting to the historical attempt to define the "real Jesus," and hence on the one hand canonical materials are denied validity, and on the other hand non-canonical materials are given precedence, e.g., the reconstructed document Q or the reconstituted *Gospel of Peter*.[21] In that way the hermeneutical function of the canon is denied, and in fact it is done quite explicitly; in this instance the people who deny it do so consciously and deliberately.

The attempt to legitimate homoerotic sexual contact as an acceptable Christian "lifestyle" is another such attempt, this time from within the confessing Christian community. Here new social and moral situations are cited, with the assurance that such situations had never crossed the purview of the authors of the canonical biblical witness, and hence their moral judgments on these matters do not need to be taken seriously.[22] In this instance, the limitations imposed by the canonical witness on certain ways of conducting a life in accord with the foundational Christian witness are themselves negated, and in that way actions can be declared acceptable which do in fact fall outside the hermeneutical limitation imposed by the canon.

---

[21] The "Jesus Seminar" is a prime example of the denial of such canonical limitations, although there are of course others.

[22] The attempt by some in the Presbyterian Church in the United States of America (PCUSA) to allow the ordination of self-avowed practicing homosexuals is a prime example of such an attempt, although there are of course others.

The current crisis in the Christian community and its witness to the foundational events upon which its life and practice are based can thus be understood in terms of a denial of the hermeneutical limitations imposed by the canon. By denying such limitations, the authoritative Christian witness can be broadened to include virtually any form of belief or practice from any source whatsoever. It is not accidental, therefore, that the authority of the scriptural witness is inextricably tied to the authority of the hermeneutical function of the canon. Without the one, the other cannot exist. Only where both are acknowledged can the life-transforming power of the scriptural witness be allowed its God-willed free reign within the Christian community. Where canonical authority is denied, Scripture becomes, in Calvin's phrase, a "nose of wax" which can be twisted into any shape desirable at any given time. At that point, the foundational events of the Christian faith are ignored, if not denied, and the result reflects cultural rather than scriptural norms. It is the case that the current confusion within "mainline" denominations in the matters of what is acceptable for faith and practice, and what is not, reflects the ignoring of canonical authority, and as a result a denial of scriptural authority. Until the authority of the canon is recovered, and with it the authority of the scriptural witness to the foundational events of the Christian community, those church bodies will continue to be characterized by the pain and frustration of a life without legitimate constraints.

Epilogue:
The Bible and the Word of God

Understanding the Bible as inspired means that this collection of writings stands in a unique relationship to the community of faith which God has called into existence and which he continues to sustain. Reflecting the struggles of the community of faith to understand itself and its role in the world, Scripture is both its product and its norm. As the product and the norm of the people God has chosen, first Israel and then the church, the Bible has a unique authority because it has been summoned forth by the Spirit as record and guide for the community of faith. Can it therefore be said to be the word of God as well?

It is regularly affirmed in some circles that in fact Scripture is the word of God, and any who would question such an equation are regarded as calling into question the inspired nature of Scripture. To be sure, Scripture contains the record of oracles which, at the time they were received, were identified as the word of God by the prophets who received them. Amos, Hosea, Isaiah, Ezekiel—the list could go on—all witness to the occurrence to them of the "word of God." Our ability to read those recorded oracles bears clear enough testimony to the fact that Scripture contains words that were identified as God's word when they were spoken.

Several points need to be kept clear, however. In the first place, those oracles of the prophets were always of immediate relevance to the situation into which they were spoken. There was apparently for the prophets no "timeless" word of God. There was only the word directly relevant to a specific situation, and then, clearly, not relevant in the same direct way to different, not to say opposite, situations. For the word of God to be the word of God, therefore, it is clear that it must be directed specifically to the situation into which it is spoken. One may distill "timeless truths" or "divine principles" from these oracles, but the word of God never occurs in such a form. It comes to specific persons at specific historical junctures and carries specific tidings about the purpose of God at that point in history.

In the second place, the only equation regarding the word of God that is found in the New Testament at least, and surely in the Bible as a whole, does not concern written Scripture, or even a verbal communication. The identification is with a person, Jesus of Nazareth, as in the opening verses of the Gospel of John. When the divine Word (John 1:1) became flesh in Jesus (v. 14), it entered the world as communication, but as communication in the form of a total event: a person who acted and was acted upon, as well as one who spoke. Again, the Word became a specific incident at a specific time and place. The Word did not become a timeless principle in Jesus of Nazareth; it became a time-bound person who lived in a specific period of time. If, however, one can say that "Jesus is the Word of God," on the basis of the biblical witness, one cannot say the same about the biblical witness itself. That witness *points* to the Word—it records the prophetic oracles and the career of Jesus of Nazareth—but in doing so it points away from itself, to the concrete occurrences of the Word of God at various junctures in history.

If that were all there were to say, then we could speak of Scripture as the witness of the Word of God, in whose pages we could find what that word was in past times. We could not say, however, that the Bible was the word of God, or even that it could become the word of God, if that word only comes with immediate relevance to the time in which it was spoken. The Bible points to the time it occurred in the past, and that would be the end of it. Yet in fact it is also as the witness of Scripture that Jesus of Nazareth became something more than a time-bound individual with the event of his resurrection from the dead. If he *was* the Word of God as Jesus of Nazareth, he *is* the Word of God as Jesus Christ, risen and regnant. As such, he can continue to communicate to us God's word for our situation. It is the intent of the doctrine of the inspiration of Scripture to affirm that in the experience of the church that is exactly what happens when the message of the biblical witness is proclaimed within the community of faith. The Spirit which vivifies the community of faith is also the Spirit who has summoned forth the words of Scripture from various junctures within the life of that community, both before and after the historical event of Jesus of Nazareth. The proclamation by that community of faith, its witness to its living Lord, can therefore be the word of God in all its timely relevance for the historic juncture at which we live. For that reason, proclamation lies at the heart of the activity of the community of faith. In this proclamation, the witness of the Scripture can once again be vivified by the same Spirit who originally summoned it forth, and in that way, it can become again for us the word of God.

For that reason, the understanding of Scripture as inspired is essential for any understanding of the role that Scripture has played and continues to play in the life and experience of the community of faith. Revivified individually and corporately by the witness of Scripture, the community of faith confesses in the doctrine of the inspiration of Scripture that the risen Christ continues to be heard, admonishing and comforting, challenging and directing the life of the community of faith as it seeks to be faithful in history to the will of the Lord of history. It is the experience of the church that Scripture has indeed become, and will continue to become, the word of God for the community of faith. It is that reality to which the doctrine of the inspiration of Scripture points.

Isaiah described the word of God as potent and sure, as incapable of failing to accomplish the purpose for which God sent it forth. That potency continues to work in the community of faith, and through it in the world at large, as the inspired Scriptures of that community of faith become again, through the continuing power of the Spirit who first summoned forth those Scriptures from the life of that community, God's word, his saving and judging word, for the times in which we live.

Index of Names and Subjects